Poetry Ireland Review 112

Eagarthóir/Editor

JOHN F DEANE

Name and Nature:
'Who Do You Say That I Am?'

Poetry Ireland Ltd/Éigse Éireann Teo gratefully acknowledges the assistance of The Arts Council/An Chomhairle Ealaíon and The Arts Council of Northern Ireland.

the arts council an chomhairle ealaíon · funding literature · artscouncil.ie

arts council of Northern Ireland · LOTTERY FUNDED

Poetry Ireland invites individuals and commercial organisations to become Friends of Poetry Ireland. For more details please contact:

Poetry Ireland Friends Scheme, Poetry Ireland, 32 Kildare St, Dublin 2, Ireland

or telephone +353 1 6789815; e-mail management@poetryireland.ie

Friends:
Joan and Joe McBreen, James Hickey, Desmond Windle, Neville Keery, Noel and Anne Monahan, Ruth Webster, Maurice Earls, Oliver Marshall, Mary Shine Thompson, Seán Coyle, Andrew Caldicott, Henry and Deirdre Comerford

Poetry Ireland Review is published three times a year by Poetry Ireland Ltd. The Editor enjoys complete autonomy in the choice of material published. The contents of this publication should not be taken to reflect either the views or the policy of the publishers.

ISBN: 1-902121-50-3
ISSN: 0332-2998

Assistant editor: Paul Lenehan (typesetting, proofreading, pre-publication) with the assistance of Peter Salisbury, Beth St John and proofreader Orla Higgins

Irish-Language Consultant: Aifric Mac Aodha
Design: Alastair Keady (**www.hexhibit.com**)

Printed in Ireland by **Brunswick Press Ltd**, Unit B2, Bluebell Industrial Estate, D13

Contents

Poetry Ireland Review 112

John F Deane	5	EDITORIAL
Pádraig J Daly	8	INCARNATION
	11	BLINDED
	12	PASSOVER
	12	PRAYER IN AGE
Maitreyabandhu	13	THE GARDEN
	14	VISITATION
	15	HOMECOMING
Pauline Stainer	16	LONG FRIDAY
Neil Curry	17	KINGFISHER
Christian Wiman	18	THE PREACHER ADDRESSES THE SEMINARIANS
Thomas Kinsella	20	TOO DIRECT FOR THIS WORLD
Gerard Smyth	21	OLD NEWS
	22	PROXIES
	23	IN THE SUPPER ROOM
Gillian Clarke	24	THE CARPENTER'S BOY
Eva Bourke	25	PIETÀ
	27	SISTER HILDEGARD AT 98 CONSIDERS HER LIFE
	28	JESUS IN MAYO
Enda McDonagh	29	ESSAY: JESUS AND POETRY
Gwyneth Lewis	39	FRUIT
Thomas McCarthy	40	IT WAS NOT OUR FAULT
Steve Ely	41	DISMAS THE GOOD THIEF
Fred Marchant	42	BEIT SAHUR
	43	A DAY LATER
	44	PARASKEVI
	45	SIXTY-SIX
Harry Clifton	46	A VISION OF HOKKAIDO IN THE RAIN
Wendell Berry	48	from A TIMBERED CHOIR
John Burnside	49	OFFICIUM
George Kalogeris	50	ICONOSTASIS
	51	ATHANASSIOS
Andrew Lansdown	53	SEHNSUCHT
	54	MEASURE
	54	PATH
	55	MAN OF SORROWS
John Ennis	56	GOING BACK FOR ALL I'D ON
Daniel Tobin	60	MOUNT OF OLIVES
Sujata Bhatt	62	FLORENCE
	64	*VIRIDITAS*: HILDEGARD AND JESUS
John Poch	68	GOOD GOD
	69	MINE
Gillian Allnutt	70	IGNOMINY
	70	TO GOD MY GOD
	71	'IT IS SNOWING'
	72	'AS IT WERE HUNGER'
Mark Patrick Hederman	73	ESSAY: BEES OF THE INVISIBLE
James Harpur	83	THE WHITE SILHOUETTE

Robert Cording	87	ADVENT STANZAS
Paul Murray	92	O MERCIFUL ONE
Michael Longley	93	PIETÀ
	93	CAROL
Ian Parks	94	LAZARUS
Ruth Padel	95	from SEVEN WORDS AND AN EARTHQUAKE
John O'Donnell	102	THE STORM
Dragan Dragojlović	103	FATHER
	104	MOTHER
	105	A DISTANT VOICE
Conor McDonough	106	ESSAY: 'OUR GAZE IS SUBMARINE'
Paul Perry	111	JESUS AS A YOUNG HUNGARIAN DEAF WOMAN …
Ned Balbo	112	DEAD MAN WALKING
William Wenthe	114	A LESSER STORY
Paddy Bushe	116	TO JESUS ON THE CROSS
Philip McDonagh	117	THE MOCKERY
	118	DE-CONSTRUCTING SILENCE
	119	RENUNCIATION
	120	HORN AND IVORY
	121	THE CHOICE OF MEDIUM
Seamus Heaney	122	THE LATECOMERS
Eiléan Ní Chuilleanáin	123	TEACHING DAILY IN THE TEMPLE
Mark Jarman	125	THE TEACHABLE MOMENT
Rowan Williams	128	STATIONS OF THE GOSPEL
David Harsent	132	TRICKSTER CHRIST
Sinéad Morrissey	134	THE SECOND COMING OF CHRIST
Armand Garnet Ruffo	136	INDIAN JESUS CHRIST, 1974
Andrew Hudgins	137	ONE EASTER
Penelope Shuttle	139	HOUR'S GHOST
	140	HOURGLASSES IN THE CHURCH AT JUKKASJÄRVI
Patricia McCarthy	142	BRIDES OF CHRIST
Michael Augustin	144	ZU DRITT / THREESOME / TRÍONÓIDÍN
Wendy Cope	146	A POEM ABOUT JESUS
Murray Bodo	147	WHITE BIRCH
Colum McCann	148	ESSAY: NAME AND NATURE …
Michael Glover	150	THE BIRTH
	151	THIS MAN
	152	IN THE IMMEDIATE AFTERMATH
	153	CARELESSLY CAREFUL
	154	THE DECISION
	155	JESUS IS LORD
	156	DEPENDING
Vincent Woods	157	ABOUT HIS BUSINESS
Tim Liardet	158	SELF-PORTRAIT WITH SHROUD AND RADIATION GHOST
Fiona Sampson	159	THE FOUR-LIMBED CROSS
Nate Klug	162	MARY MAGDALENE
Dennis O'Driscoll	163	UPDATE
Notes on Contributors	165	

Editorial

There can be no doubt that Jesus, the Christ, and the Christian movement, have had enormous influence on the lives and thinking of millions of people for the last two millennia, and – particularly in the West – on the literature. In our own time, poets like R S Thomas, Geoffrey Hill, David Gascoyne and many more, were rooted to the question, as it has been posed by Walter Kasper: 'The decisive question for Christianity has always been "Who do you think Christ is? Who is he?" Answers to this question are very varied, not only in later history but even in the New Testament. Jesus has many names in the New Testament. He is called Christ, Prophet, Son of man, Servant of God, High Priest, Saviour, Lord (*Kyrios*), Son of God. Evidently no single title is adequate to indicate who Jesus is. Jesus is the man who fits no formula.' (*Jesus the Christ*, Walter Kasper, T and T Clark International, 2011).

Faith is not merely a matter of the mind, not something seen and accepted intellectually as fact or truth; faith is accepting a bond with God by means of searching. It is not something accepted once and for all, and adhered to. To be a Christian is to be continually searching through and with the words and life of Christ; if one can call oneself a Christian at the end of one's days, that is a blessing; just as one may call oneself a poet only at the end of one's life, if a certain level of poetry has been achieved. There is always doubt, there are always unanswered questions, nor is there one definitive path to be followed as every individual's experience in life is different. Hence, rules and regulations belong to different Churches like the rules of a club; differences in the degree and the kind of faith held depend, too, on different experiences. Certainty is not achievable; authoritarianism is inimical to honest individual response; as Tennyson wrote in 'In Memoriam A.H.H.':

> Perplext in faith, but pure in deeds,
>   At last he beat his music out.
>   There lives more faith in honest doubt,
> Believe me, than in half the creeds.

If faith is a question of will, of deciding for or against God, then that may well be a question of the heart. If that is the case, then it is clear that poetry and the work of the imagination play a part.

I have always felt that ours may well be a good time to find a new range of poems that face up the topic of Christ and his relevance, or otherwise, to our distraught generations. For some time I also felt that the idea might well be a foolish one, too demanding, irrelevant. On a day in

October 2010, I decided to try, for the first time in my life, to climb Croagh Patrick, 'the Reek'; I was then 67 years old and, though I was born in the shadow of the pilgrims' mountain, I had never climbed. I found it very difficult. Half-way up and the rain and mist began to drive across the mountain like a slow herd of grey horses and I could scarcely see in front of my face. The last part of the climb is truly difficult, the stones loose, the shale and larger stones just waiting for the pilgrim's one slip. But I made it to the top. The mists were dense; I could scarcely see the small chapel above. When I found it, it was, of course, shut. I leaned back against the wall for shelter, dreading the start back down. I tried to pray. I was too tired. From somewhere came the notion that here I would make my decision about the poems: I would ask someone who knows poetry and knows faith if the idea might work; I chose the then Archbishop of Canterbury, Rowan Williams, with whom I had already been in touch. I would ask him. If he thought the idea would work, then I would go ahead. If not ... well, nothing lost. I wrote to him the next day. His response was immediate, encouraging, and laden with suggestions of poets I might ask. I began the work.

I specified, when seeking these poems, that they were not to be Church, nor devotional. I do not mean that I am seeking a Christ without Church, to do away with the religious rituals and rites. But with such Church negativities and heartbreak over the last decades, I thought it might be possible and necessary to find a 'worldly holiness', as Dietrich Bonhoeffer put it, to rediscover a loving and meaningful Jesus for our times. Bonhoeffer tried not to limit his awareness of Christ. He did not ask questions such as 'Can Christ be both man and God?' He sought rather to answer the question 'Lord, who are you?' His attempt was to bring Christ into the centre, to listen, and answer Christ himself and Christ's question to us all: 'Who do you say that I am?' For Bonhoeffer it was the structures of religion that were dangerous, and they were (and are) so because they may cloud the clearer consideration of Christ. Structures may well be necessary, in the sense that 'religion' may help to back up 'faith', but it is when the structures take over from faith in Christ that damage occurs.

The poetry of faith is as vital as any other poetry, such as anti-war poetry, or political poetry, or nature poetry, or love poetry: provided the poems are excellent as poetry, for it is not ideas that make the poem. So I asked for a personal response to the person of Jesus, whether that response be positive or negative.

This gathering of poems is its own agenda; there is no prediction; there is no argument. As Thomas Merton wrote: 'Let us be proud of the words that are given to us for nothing, not to teach anyone, not to confute anyone, not to prove anyone absurd, but to point beyond all objects into the silence where nothing can be said.' So I wish to let these pieces stand, in all their personal and artistic honesty, just as they are. I am happy to have initiated and received some of the final work of the late Dennis O'Driscoll and Seamus Heaney. I am grateful to Poetry Ireland for allowing me this opportunity, in the last issue of which I am to be editor. I allow the prose pieces to stand in all their speculative questioning. And I am deeply grateful to all the poets who responded so generously to my initial request for new work. I owe a great debt of gratitude to Philip McDonagh who, as Ambassador to Russia, introduced me to the work of the modern iconographer, Valentina Aleksandrovna Zhogova.

– John F Deane, Easter 2014

Pádraig J Daly

INCARNATION

1.
We would have done it otherwise:

We would have kept the fluttering messengers,
The journey in haste,
The wondrous birth.

Pity is important;
So we would have allowed him pain
And pity.

We would have kept the feasting,
The sinner companions,
The softness of God.

But what need was there
For the garden agony, the nails through the palms,
The roars from the cross?

2.
Feeling as men and women feel,
Quaking before pain
As men and women quake,

He entrusts Himself to the High Father
As men and women trust themselves
To human constancy;

And, trusting still that luminous love,
He edges on
To the blind halt of death.

3.
That all of this – sun, water's rush,
Men and women moving, haloed, through the streets –
Came from nothing, nowhere, nobody,
I cannot credit; so believe.

It is afterwards I baulk:
Mind-melting-Otherness?
Or Otherness-Made-Flesh,
Softly among us?

4.
And, being man,

Did he think, as men and women thought,
That Jonah dwelt three days within the whale,
Immune to belly juices?

That devils lived flamboyantly inside the sick
And, when his heart was moved to heal,
Left them, yelping?

That the world soon,
With hail and lightning bolt,
Must end?

How did he foresee
The horror of his dying,
The direful future of Jerusalem?

And how much grasp unknowable God,
Bending in his flesh
To pitch among us?

5.
With human arms
Grappling each of myriad us to human heart,
There stilling us,

The love that flows from Father-God,
And all God's joy,
Holds each of us, through Him,

In an embrace,
Where every doltish one of us
Is marvellous and singular,

Where there is no longer need
For talk or explanation, gestures of regret;
Just simple surrender to our God's delight.

Pádraig J Daly

BLINDED

After all the years of holding up the bread,
Calling attention to the presence,
After all the years of welcoming the freshly fledged
Beneath Your shelter,

After all the years of listening in Your stead
To chronicles of wrong,
Offering comprehension;
And years of pleas for wisdom, healing,

After years of digging through
The arguments of Palestine,
Presenting, astonished over,
Those parables of joy,

After all the years of reaching in Your name
To sick and halt, the dying and the dead,
Your Godness blinds me yet
To who You are.

Pádraig J Daly

PASSOVER

All across the city,
The fevered bleating of lambs;
And, then, the noises of slaughter!

Blood everywhere – in halls, in kitchens,
On doors, on lintels,
Spattered over the people!

And so they lead him,
Impotent animal,
Into the gore.

PRAYER IN AGE

Let me trust You, Lord, to the going-out of my days.

When I am led again in halterstrings,
Grant that I be led kindly:
Do not abandon me to derision.

When nights are dark
And I have no strength, even to pray,
Do not cast me off.

Lead me to those fields
Where every sheep is known by name.
Let me be as rain, disappearing, on Your ocean.

Maitreyabandhu

THE GARDEN

After we did it under the hedge
where two hawthorns met
near the cooking-apple tree
and the wreck of the Austin Princess,
I ran down the April garden

past my father's potato drills.
I knew it was wrong. I ran.
And under cherry blossom
between the tomato greenhouse
and another pile of scrap

I nearly collided with my mom
coming from the washing line,
her basket full of sunny sheets
and brothers' shirts, her arms
freckled with (how I saw it) love.

That night I prayed to Jesus.
He was standing on a hill
surrounded by animals – two lambs,
a goat, a flock of sparrows.
I prayed no one would ever know.

Maitreyabandhu

VISITATION

Strange that you should come
like that, without any form at all,
carrying no symbolic implements,
without smile or frown
or any commotion,
as if you had been there all the time,
like a pair of gloves left in a pocket.

As if I had been looking *that* way,
into the wide blue yonder, and you were
beside me, enduring my hard luck stories
with infinite patience. Not even waiting –
the tree outside my window
doesn't wait, nor the ocean-wedge
with its new, precise horizon – just *there*
like the shadow of a church

or a quiet brother.
And how I saw you, in the mess of things,
was as a slant of grey,
the perfect grey of house dust,
an absolute neutral, with no weaving,
no shimmer of cobalt
and light-years away from Byzantium.

Grey. And I want to add, like light,
as if a skylight opened in my skull,
and into the darkness fell
a diagonal of pure Bodmin Moor.
But even that's too bright,
too world-we're-busy-in.
Call it 'dust' then, or the bloom
of leaf-smoke from an autumn fire.

Maitreyabandhu

HOMECOMING

If I had to think of a place,
          I'd think of those cold shallows
                    where the dogs drank
and I threw a stick
and everything was patterned with sycamore.
          I'd think of myself as a child
                    falling asleep
in the back of the Austin Princess.

I'd think of our being together
                    as a small thing –
picking up a windfall
          or pouring a tumblerful of water –
                    the moment, extended,
when an engine stops and time folds away.

You were blurred,
                    as though through chlorine –
your rose-body wavered,
          breaking up,
                    your limbs made ripples
when I spoke.

          We were there together.
And it might have been
          at the top of the garden
near the hole-in-the-hedge,
          or it might have been anywhere
between traffic noise,
          in the Sunday silence of the high street.

Authors's Note: 'Visitation' and 'Homecoming', both directly inspired by Buddhism, are attempts to communicate something of my meditation practice – especially my experience of meditating on an archetypal form of the Buddha from the Tibetan tradition, called *Padmasambhava*. This ideal image is contemplated in order to cultivate an affinity between my own unenlightened state and the goal of Buddhist practice.

Pauline Stainer

LONG FRIDAY

1

Small sun through mist,
five turbines in silverpoint
blades turning, turning,
a swish as of walking
through long grass.

Then the eerie shift
of something unfinished,
flicker-shadow,
the uncoordinated wounds
of Christ.

2

Crucifixion,
a centurion
gazing up at the body
with its crown
of razor-wire

transfixed by
that shimmer
in zero-sunlight –
incarnation,
the dove

in the double helix.

Neil Curry

KINGFISHER

If Christ our king could
In the ammoniac stench of the stable
Suffer at His Nativity to be
Neighbour to slow-breathing beasts,

Then small wonder that the king-
fisher's spark should be struck
In a damp underworld of willow root and worm
Where vole and water-rat splash.

For once the shells split and sapphire
And fire-opal fledge in their filth
And six or seven small spurts of flame
Are tumbled out into the dazzle,

Then earth, air, fire and water meet
In a perfection of balance, trafficking,
Like prayer, between this world and that.
And isn't it then that their mother's

Fabled and other self is said to brood
On a nest of bones, calming the waters,
And granting us glimpses of Eden
In those Mary-blue halcyon days?

Christian Wiman

THE PREACHER ADDRESSES THE SEMINARIANS

I tell you it's a bitch existence some Sundays
and it's no good pretending you don't have to pretend,

don't have to hitch up those gluefutured nags Hope and Help
and whip the sorry chariot of yourself

toward whatever Hell your Heaven is on days like these.
I tell you it takes some hunger Heaven itself won't slake

to be so twitchingly intent on the pretty organist's pedaling,
so lizardly alert to the curvelessness of her choir robe.

Here it comes, brothers and sisters, the confession of sins,
hominy hominy, dipstick doxology, one more churchcurdled hymn

we don't so much sing as haunt: grounded altos, gear-grinding
  tenors,
three score and ten gently bewildered men lip-synching along.

You're up, Pastor. Bring on the unthunder. Some trickle-piss tangent
to reality. Some bit of the Gospel grueling out of you.

I tell you sometimes mercy means nothing
but release from this homiletic hologram, a little fleshstep

sideways, as it were, setting passion on autopilot (as if it weren't!)
to gaze out in peace at your peaceless parishioners:

boozeglazes and facelifts, bad mortgages, bored marriages,
a masonry of faces at once specific and generic,

and here and there that rapt famished look that leaps
from person to person, year to year, like a holy flu.

All these little crevices into which you've crawled
like a chubby plumber with useless tools:

Here, have a verse for your wife's death.
Here, have a death for your life's curse.

I tell you some Sundays even the children's sermon
– maybe especially this – sharks your gut

like a bite of tin some beer-guzzling goat
either drunkenly or mistakenly decides to sample.

I know what you're thinking. Christ's in this.
He'll get to it, the old cunner, somewhere somehow

there's the miracle meat, the aurora borealis blood,
every last atom compacted to a grave

and the one thing that every man must lose to save.
Well friends, I'm here to tell you two things today.

First, though this is not, for me, one of those bilious abrading days,
though in fact I stand before you in a rage of faith

and have all good hope that you will all go help
untold souls back into their bodies,

ease the annihilating No above which they float,
the truth is our only saviour is failure.

Which brings me to the second thing: that goat.
It was real. It is, as is usually the case, the displacement of agency

that is the lie. It was long ago, Mexico, my demon days:
It was a wager whose stakes I failed to appreciate.

He tottered. He flowered. He writhed time to a fraught quiet,
and kicked occasionally, and twitched, and watched me die.

Thomas Kinsella

TOO DIRECT FOR THIS WORLD

> We are all of us born in moral stupidity.
> – George Eliot, *Middlemarch*

> You must love your neighbour as yourself.
> – Christ: moral genius

*

The records differ in detail, but all are agreed
on His nature as a man: compassionate and precise
in His judgment of men's conduct;
arrogant and gentle in fatal combination.
Torn from the flesh in carnal pantomime
– too direct for this world.

Records of the last meal show the early signs
of theatre, as the courtesies formed themselves
under their otherworldly burden
into the first outline of a sacrament ...

– first published in *Love Joy Peace* (Peppercanister 29)

Gerard Smyth

OLD NEWS

All through childhood I faced the wounds of Christ
and counted five. The crown of thorns
was just a centurion's jibe. But what endures is the long,
loud orphaned cry, his abandoned voice
calling out to the God-of-no-reply –
another Isaac forsaking his own son,
letting him hang there over the abyss,
on a cross of coarsened wood
(not like the smooth and polished stuff
in every church). There was nothing to say,
the women wept and someone recorded every detail
of the facts; the details have not changed since then:
Bethlehem, Jerusalem, a woodworker's son.
It is old news now, the Easter mystery of the tomb,
of the stone rolled back, a stone that only strong men
could move that morning in the dark before time resumed.

Gerard Smyth

PROXIES

Searching for God is the first thing and the last,
but in between such trouble, and such pain.
– Jane Kenyon

Some days your whereabouts is a mystery.
You send your proxies among us.
The wild man on the Jesus channel, the preacher
who hands out guilt and robs our mirth.

In those rags you wear
you raise a paper cup that barely tinkles.
You are the stumbling roughneck, druggy-eyed,
dressed in runners and a tracksuit.

You are the pusher at the school gate,
the worthless father who beats his wife.
You could be any age, in many guises: a widow
of the parish whose children vanish when she weeps,

a lawbreaker, a commander-in-chief,
graceful or grotesque – perhaps the misshapen
heap among embankment trees,
waiting there to catch the falling bird;

or are you the actor on the stage six nights a week
in the *Theatre of the Absurd*?

Gerard Smyth

IN THE SUPPER ROOM

Never did learn to drink that blood and call it wine.
– Bob Dylan

When our guide mentioned that we had entered
the room of the Last Supper
I stood in a trance until I remembered
I had to be somewhere else …

… but not before I wondered
who brought the wine, who broke the bread
and divided it and where exactly did Judas sit
counting the hours to his Judas-kiss
and tender whispers of endearment.

The room was not one I recognised
from works of the Old Masters
and not one painted in the colours of the Renaissance.
But plain and dull, yet suitable
for a mealtime rendezvous.

In the trees outside, still visible
in the darkening hour, songbirds of the bible
were singing loudly.
And I thought of Jesus counting the hours
that took him closer to Friday.

Gillian Clarke

THE CARPENTER'S BOY

They used to call him 'little solemn one'
when he didn't gurgle at their sing-song words,
but lay awake in his shawl, staring at them.
Always awake. I worried. He didn't cry
or laugh. His gaze would hold an adult's eye
until they flinched and looked away.

Before he could walk he loved the workshop,
the tools and wood his toys. Sawdust
in a shaft of sunlight made him wonder,
and when wood uncurled from the plane
to lie in yellow piles, he'd cry for me to
Look! Look! Angel's hair!

Sharp tools were not allowed. Dangerous.
He gathered small things, a cube of sandalwood,
the planed handle of a box, and once,
I prised bright metal from his curled fingers,
silver in sunlight on his open palm,
from the workshop floor, three nails.

Years later, when we lost and found him, just a boy
holding a crowd in thrall, or raging in the temple,
turning bankers from the house of God,
when he lived wild, wore rags, preached socialism,
consorted with disease and poverty,
I remembered his small hand, those toys.

Eva Bourke

PIETÀ

Whoever humbles himself as this little child
is the greatest in the kingdom of heaven.
– Matthew 18:4

Behold, children are a heritage from the Lord.
– Psalm 127:3

Last night I saw Jesus on television. We had changed from a discussion on obesity, crash diets, healthy nutrition to another channel and she was there, Jesus, a girl of six on a stinking mountain of rubbish somewhere in the Philippines. She was having her hair washed by her mother before a day of work foraging in the dump. Jesus, her mother, her six siblings and many women and children like them, lived on the garbage mountain in shacks made of rusted corrugated iron, wooden planks and cardboard, every bit salvaged from the dump. This was no 'slum of hope'.

When she was born, there was neither manger nor oxen, no donkeys nor shepherds with flocks of well-fed sheep, and the angelic choruses were silent. Jesus had never tasted honey, nor bitten into a tomato, nor heard of apples. As soon as she could walk she foraged for scraps of foul food in the shifting rotting mass with other children who also didn't know what an apple was, who had never seen a toy or a playground. The rats in the stinking pile were large as cats, and violet flies covered the children's faces as they worked in the heat and stench, digging up to their elbows in slimy refuse for anything of value, nails, coke cans, shreds of plastic. Jesus' hair was crawling with lice, her stomach pained from hunger and there were sores around her mouth. Bulldozers that pushed down and flattened the rubbish before depositing new heaps, sometimes rolled over a child.

How can I write about Jesus, who may have been the son of God, the son of a Roman soldier, the son of a carpenter and his wife Mary, born around the time when Pontius Pilatus was governor in Israel around two millennia ago? Who may have studied the Talmud, been a rabbi, a fisherman, a prophet, who frequented the houses of outcasts, spoke up for sinners, attacked the rich, loved children, performed miracles, who was said to be wise, good, contrary, who pitied the poor and was a terrorist? Who was captured, tortured, crucified, died for us, rose from the dead? We crucify Jesus daily a thousand times over on stinking mountains, in favelas running with open sewers, in arid wastes without water, in platoons of child soldiers. Our superfast trading computers, Sniper or Stealth, transfer billions across the globe in split seconds, they drive up the price of the grain they hoard in their stores, they gamble away children, humming contentedly, bees in a high-rise hive running with gold. There will always be enough rubbish to feed Jesus and many like her, anaemic, undersized, hungry, an army of skeletal shadows on the banks of a filthy Styx, far from the place where the living dwell.

Let the children sleep in the sky. Let them taste honey from flowers, give them windmills of flowers, the sweet milk of the wild sheep. Let them dream of clear water washing their wounds, a cool wind rising and blessing their foreheads. Jesus' mother weeps over her crucified child. Have you forsaken her, too, father? Can you forgive us, although we do know what we do?

Eva Bourke

SISTER HILDEGARD AT 98 CONSIDERS HER LIFE

As a girl, all I wanted was to be a parachutist
like Lilly Byczkowsky, my heroine –
afloat, a tiny figure in the centre of a silken bell, airlifted
into the high blue theatre of the sky –
or a pilot, a flight traffic controller, anything
to do with the heavens. I wanted to know

what was going on there. I still do. Nightly
I stand by the window of my cell – girded
and ready in my black tunic, cingulum, white veil, black veil –
and watch the planes, those metallic science-fiction angels,
go round in circles above Frankfurt airport, hear them growl
evangels at the lit-up city below.

You agnostics sadden me, how will you ever
grasp what happened. I was young, fiery, the tapestries
were spread out before me with their streams and
forests of wild beasts. Why I did not enter them?
A voice called, come, what could I do? I said, Jesus, surely
not me, not now, not yet. But I went, just like that. I fell

without even a parachute to hold on to, I fell in love, taking
the thermals on trust. And what for? A niche in the cemetery wall?
Was it all worth it, the chilly vespers with the sisters, more a cantata
  of coughs
than hosannas, icy winter mornings in the steamed-up convent laundry,
chilblains, years of fasting and obedience? The mysterious rustle of
  habit fabrics,
the whispered envious gossip, soot and alabaster in altarpieces,

baroque clouds and the eyes of the Saviour picked out with gold
leaf? I, too, saw blood seeping from embroideries and bell towers
  ablaze
with stigmata. But all this is long past.
Empty, scoured, almost transparent as parachute silk,
I am only the conduit through which blessings pass
from him to me to you and you – watch out, pass them on.

Eva Bourke

JESUS IN MAYO

Too far distant to be sure as the bus
lurches and slows at the T-junction in the driving rain
whether the whitish figure hanging between
the trees at the back of playing fields
is the fleet afterimage of some murderous *après-midi*
sacrifice, some rushed, hushed-up afternoon
mob's blood-sports near the god-forsaken
hard shoulder where potholed, drizzle-slickened country
roads join in a cross of sorts and no sane man
in his right mind would intervene nor kneel
before his open-armed Do Not Pass appeal,
bestowing blessings of smudged ashes
and rain on foreheads, a roadside
saviour, resin and gypsum, bemired and moss-
streaked and what's more barely held together by
chicken-wire and plaster of Paris bandages.
I ask you, Jesus in Mayo-God-help-us, have mercy
and bless us for better or worse, turn
towards us and bless this evening that's washed out
on bus shelter roofs and tarmac in small town
squares, bless the Thai Orchard Take Away
the Golden Seas chipper, the Coffee-to-Go café,
the Last Reductions Emporium, the billboard
commanding Walk the Walk, the Swallow's Nest
Public House and the Eye Candy Properties, not least
their proprietor Mr Louis T Lynx and the man on his ladder
in white overalls who's fixing a street-
lamp, the empty boom time villas, the White Cow water
tower and the hooded crows that scatter
from the tower like wet grape shot, bless villages, hills
hedgerows and farms with their steaming barns
the T-Junction and the sodden playing fields
the county colours – red and green – and the yellow letters
painted on the road SLOW VERY,
the intercom that tells us again and again
please stand clear when doors open,
bless plaster, paint and resin
the poor and raw materials of our adoration
and incense, blood and bitumen.

Enda McDonagh

JESUS AND POETRY

In a life-long struggle with Christian theology, in my efforts to understand and live and so teach the Gospel of Jesus Christ, I have been helped in significant ways by poets, living and dead, believing and non-believing, even by those who might be happy to accept the self-description of the late and very much lamented Dennis O Driscoll, 'disbelieving non-believer'.

For me, and I believe for many theologians, the Gospel of Jesus Christ as recorded in the New Testament, explored and witnessed over two millennia, offers continuing insight into the human condition, its strengths and weaknesses, its potential for good and evil, its origins and destiny. From its quite different starting-points and stand-points in all its wonderful variations, real poetry exposes many of the same human dimensions in confirmation and critique. This brief essay seeks to explore how that mutual confirmation and critique of poetry and Gospel in dialogue have enriched this particular Christian believer and non-poet over his six decades plus of adult life. A few reservations are in order.

A loving reader of poetry over the past six decades and more, I never received that higher education in literature which would have equipped me with the historical background and technical expertise which might have set me on the way to becoming a professional literary critic. As a would-be theoretical physicist who became eventually immersed in the parallel complexities of philosophy and theology, my ventures into writing about poets and poetry might at their best be described as 'love letters'. As part of a dialogue with theology, love letters between the two great 'spirit-laden' loves of my life, if not unduly pretentious or arrogant, might then be an appropriate description. The second reservation concerns the further obvious limitation that no individual can cover as much of the poetic or theological traditions that might make a serious contribution to the dialogue envisaged here. This is especially true of somebody of my restricted literary education compounded by an increasingly declining memory. So for example the growing accessibility in original languages and in translation of 'foreign language poetry' which might be important in the proposed dialogue, must be left aside here. Similarly little of the ancient classics, valuable as they were in my earlier education, will feature. More recent English-language poetry will necessarily predominate and of that only select and more beloved pieces.

THE PARTNERS AND THE PROCESS

The partners at this initial stage of the dialogue are perhaps best identified as the poet and the reader-commentator. As their dialogue proceeds the theme and style, words, images and rhythm of various poems and poets encounter the spiritual/intellectual capacities of this theological reader in a developing 'embrace'. In another favourite metaphor the reader, attentive, sensitive and persistent is increasingly inhabited by the poem. Just so was the poet in his writing inhabited by the particular theme, words, images and music. The poet's work is labelled creative as it brings something new and different into the world. In that process he is himself changed, while the affected reader is also changed by this new arrival in his interior life. The dialogue brings fresh and loving life to both partners in sharing the poem's beauty but not without pain and labour for both partners, as W B Yeats emphasised in his fine poem: 'Adam's Curse'. The Yeats title and theme are useful reminders of my primary task, some reflection on the relationship between Jesus and Poetry as it emerges in sacred and secular literature with due regard to my own inadequacies to the task.

JESUS AND POETRY IN THE NEW TESTAMENT

The New Testament or the Bible as a whole, despite the influence of some translations and passages, does not strictly speaking qualify as a work of poetry. There are accounts of episodes, of people and dialogues, and narrative passages which have at least a poetic aura in language and image, style and imagination which enables the believer to encounter Jesus poetically, as human word en route to a theological encounter with the Word of God in faith, hope and love. Many of these passages have proved valuable sources for their poems for poets, unbelieving as well as believing, and without any necessary theological implications for either.

For all the scholarly disputes over the historical accuracy of the nativity narratives in the Gospels of Luke and Matthew, there seems to me no doubt about their poetic feel. From the message of the angel to Mary through the visit to cousin Elizabeth and so to Bethlehem, the heavenly choirs and the earthly shepherds, the gift-bearing Magi and the murderous Herod, the flight into Egypt and return to Nazareth where the child grew in wisdom and grace: the truth and the beauty, the gift and the threat integral to human existence are revealed poetry-wise. In the transforming language and insight of the poems, 'Benedictus' and 'Magnificat', the divine dimensions of the narrative reach us in explicit poetic form. This Jesus was born of poetry, of its creative Word, divine and human.

There are many other narrative passages with similar implicit poetic potential including the meal miracles, the story of the woman taken in adultery and the event of the transfiguration. Obviously the most powerful are the various accounts of the betrayal, trial, passion and death to which we will return. The parables and the Sermon on the Mount in language, lesson and imagination offer the persuasions, insights and imagery of poetry in the teaching ministry of Jesus as appropriate to its central message of love, the first and greatest commandment. The development of this teaching in the farewell discourses in the Gospel of John (plus the Pauline hymn in I Corinthians) carry the passion and power of great rhetoric in its close kinship with poetry. All these aspects of Jesus' relationship to poetry in his life and ministry are laid bare in Australian James McAuley's 'An Art of Poetry', dedicated to his fellow Australian Vincent Buckley.

> If all our keys are lost or broken
> Shall it be thought absurd
> If for an art of words I turn
> Discreetly to the Word?
>
> Drawn inward by his love, we trace
> Art to its secret springs:
> What, are we Masters in Israel
> And do not know these things?
>
> Lord Christ from out his treasury
> Brings forth things new and old:
> We have these treasures in earthen vessels,
> In parables he told,
>
> And in the single images
> Of seed, and fish, and stone,
> Or, shaped in deed and miracle,
> To living poems grown.
>
> [...]
>
> Give every image space and air
> To grow, or as a bird to fly;
> So shall one grain of mustard seed
> Quite overspread the sky.
>
> [...]

We know, where Christ has set his hand
Only the real remains:
I am impatient for that loss
By which the spirit gains.

The culmination of all four Gospel accounts is the Passion narratives. Although the Resurrection forms the climactic conclusion to the life and death of Jesus, from an artistic viewpoint the Passion carries the greater power. This is borne out by the preoccupation of so many diverse artists and arts with that passion and death in poetry, painting and music. One of the earliest poetic responses in the English language tradition is the eighth century poem 'The Dream of the Rood', subject of many later versions in modern English, including one by contemporary Irish poet, John F Deane. Before reflecting on later literature I take a brief look at the New Testament writings, particularly the Gospels, and their own poetic impact in word and image, in structure and rhythm.

McAuley's strategy of tracing 'Art to its secret springs' enables us to see Jesus as teacher, even moral instructor, invoking a poetic style in the direct instruction of the Sermon on the Mount, or the great commandments of love, or indirectly but still more powerfully in the parables of the Forgiving Father (aka the Prodigal Son) and of the Good Samaritan, among so many others. One might contrast the Eight Beatitudes as they are called with the language and tone of the Ten Commandments reflecting in turn the different personalities of their human authors as poets and legislators. The person of Jesus and his ministry of compassion in healing the sick and forgiving sinners prompts one contemporary scripture scholar (José Antonio Pagola) to speak of 'The Poet of Compassion'. Not only in his explicit teaching, but in his ministry and in the story of his life and death, the poet and the poem that is Jesus reaches us as we read. Through these very Gospels and the further New Testament writings they reached the community of believers (the ecclesia) over the millennia. As McAuley suggests, it is in this story of creation and reconciliation, summarised so powerfully in the prologue to St John's Gospel and in the opening verses of St Paul's Letter to the Colossians that we find the 'secret springs' not just of poetry but of all art. From the earliest years of Christianity then in word and sacrament, in painting and sculpture, in music and song, in prayer and liturgy, we find these hidden traces which have pervaded Western civilisation ever since.

'The Dream of the Rood' is an early example of a vernacular work which captures so beautifully and imaginatively a central aspect of this all-encompassing artistic tradition. Its imaginative distinctiveness arises from the narrator-tree telling of its role in the Crucifixion of Jesus. Its theological distinctiveness arises from its Pauline character as speaking for all creation and not just humanity in the story of redemption; nature crying out for and finding salvation in and through the same Jesus Christ, becoming Paul's New Creation.

> I was raised up a Rood, carrying the powerful King ...
>
> ... They pierced me with bloody nails, the pain still stings!
>
> [...]
>
> [A]ll of creation mourned, moaned this cruel chance:
>
> And Christ was on the Rood.

The Rood itself shared then in the glorification of Christ in resurrection with all humanity and all nature in the New Creation, as Paul 'Christened' it.

The death and resurrection of Jesus recur as poetic subjects over the centuries particularly in medieval hymns such as '*Vexilla Regis*' and other liturgical forms. One of my favourite modern versions is by twentieth century English poet David Gascoyne, which follows the outline of a Mass. Entitled '*Miserere*' it appeared in the volume *Poems* 1937-1942. Just as 'The Dream of the Rood' drew the whole of creation into the salvation of Christ on the Cross, so Gascoyne's poem illuminates for us the continuing act of New Creation by Christ on the Rood. This is most clearly developed in the final poem of the sequence, 'Ecce Homo':

> Whose is this horrifying face,
> This putrid flesh, discoloured, flayed ...
>
> ... Behold the Man: He is Man's Son.
>
> [...]
>
> Lest the great scandal be no more disguised:
> He is in agony till the world's end,
>
> [...]
>
> And He must watch this drama to the end.
>
> [...]

Not from a monstrance silver-wrought
But from the tree of human pain
Redeem our sterile misery,
Christ of Revolution and of Poetry,
That man's long journey through the night
May not have been in vain.

The 'Christ of Revolution and of Poetry' is an inspiring call to many, including myself, provided the revolution is understood in non-violent terms, and the transformation is that of the Justice and Peace promised and called for in the Reign of God announced by Jesus. Interestingly, the Irish independence revolution initiated early in the twentieth century owed much to the Irish literary movement promoted by W B Yeats, many of its key figures were recalled in his poem 'Easter 1916'. Among these were poets like Thomas MacDonagh, 'He might have won fame in the end', and Joseph Mary Plunkett, whose best known poem – 'I See His Blood Upon the Rose' – discerned the presence of Jesus in the natural world, echoing 'The Dream of the Rood', Wordsworth's *Tintern Abbey*, and Gascoyne's crucifixion language:

I see his blood upon the rose
And in the stars the glory of his eyes,
His body gleams amid eternal snows,
His tears fall from the skies.

The connection between revolution and poetry also attributed to Wordsworth in his Tintern Abbey days is sharply differentiated as Christian by Plunkett and others from the seeming pantheism of the Wordsworth world of poets.

The companionship of Jesus on the Cross emerges in unusual and unexpected ways in a variety of poems and poets. 'Lightenings, xii', from Seamus Heaney's collection *Seeing Things*, I find especially attractive:

And lightening? One meaning of that
Beyond the usual sense of alleviation,
Illumination, and so on, is this:

A phenomenal instant when the spirit flares
With pure exhilaration before death –
The good thief in us harking to the promise!

So paint him on Christ's right hand, on a promontory
Scanning empty space, so body-racked he seems
Untranslatable into the bliss

> Ached for at the moon-rim of his forehead,
> By nail-craters on the dark side of his brain:
> *This day thou shalt be with Me in Paradise.*

Nine months after his death, in the context of his final text-message to his wife Marie – *Noli Timere* (Be not afraid) – it reads more movingly still.

R S Thomas, Anglican clergyman and gifted poet of the dark, encounters Jesus on the Cross while attending a concert by violinist Fritz Kreisler, 'So near that I could see the toil / Of his face muscles ... I could see, too, the twitching of the fingers ... / This player who so beautifully suffered / For each of us upon his instrument ... / So it must have been on Calvary / In the fiercer light of the thorns' halo ... / The hands bleeding, the mind bruised but calm, / Making such music as lives still. / and no one daring to interrupt / Because it was himself that he played / And closer than all of them the God listened.'

Among the great poetic narratives of the Gospels the Nativity journey of the three kings and the post-Resurrection journey of the two disciples from Jerusalem to Emmaus stand out for me as hymns of closure and disclosure in their birth-death (of Jesus and the Holy Innocents) and death-(re)birth of Jesus as the wholly innocent.

T S Eliot's poem 'Journey of the Magi' offers a magisterial retelling of the Gospel story that is the Magi's story, and yet also the story of Jesus the Incarnate God, enduring the suffering of a man at the hands of man – indeed the story of every man from birth to death. The 'cold coming' in which it all begins, the refractory company, human and animal, the hostility of cities, towns and villages, the final relief in the 'temperate valley' with the threat of the three trees on the horizon and the hands dicing at the inn door. Arriving not a moment too soon and yet finding the place unsatisfactory. All a long time ago and yet not sure if that long journey was for birth or death. A birth certainly but different: ' ... this Birth was hard and bitter agony for us, like Death, our death'; 'We returned to our places' but no longer at home'; 'I should be glad of another death.'

The complexity, power and darkness in Eliot's poem, in place of what we might have expected to follow the angels' celebratory song, is in marked contrast to Denise Levertov's brief, simple and joyful Easter poem 'The Servant-Girl at Emmaus (A Painting by Velázquez)':

> She listens, listens, holding
> her breath. Surely that voice
> is his – the one
> who had looked at her, once, across the crowd,
> as no one ever had looked?
> Had seen her? Had spoken as if to her?
>
> [...]

Those who had brought this stranger home to their table
don't recognise yet with whom they sit.
But she in the kitchen, absently touching
the winejug she's to take in
a young Black servant intently listening,

swings round and sees
the light around him
and is sure.

The rich heritage of the Western Christian Tradition even today in its dominantly secular frame offers an impossible array of poems directly and indirectly invoking, encountering and revealing Jesus. Some of the most beautiful and arresting in the English language tradition are by George Herbert and Gerald Manley Hopkins. Two of their best loved may be Herbert's 'Love (III)' and Hopkins's 'As Kingfishers Catch Fire'. They complement each other in an interesting way for the purposes of this essay on Jesus and poetry:

LOVE III

Love bade me welcome; yet my soul drew back,
Guilty of dust and sin.
But quick-eyed Love, observing me grow slack
From my first entrance in,
Drew nearer to me, sweetly questioning
If I lacked anything.

'A guest,' I answered, 'worthy to be here';
Love said, 'You shall be he.'
'I, the unkind, ungrateful? Ah, my dear
I cannot look on Thee.'
Love took my hand, and smiling did reply,
'Who made the eyes but I?'

'Truth, Lord, but I have marred them; let my shame
Go where it doth deserve.'
'And know you not,' says Love, 'who bore the blame?'
'My dear, then I will serve.'
'You must sit down,' says Love, 'and taste my meat.'
So I did sit and eat.

AS KINGFISHERS CATCH FIRE

As kingfishers catch fire, dragonflies draw flame;
As tumbled over rim in roundy wells
Stones ring; like each tucked string tells, each hung bell's
Bow swung finds tongue to fling out broad its name;
Each mortal thing does one thing and the same:
Deals out that being indoors each one dwells;
Selves – goes itself, *myself* it speaks and spells,
Crying *What I do is me: for that I came.*

I say more: the just man justices;
Keeps grace: that keeps all his goings graces;
Acts in God's eye what in God's eye he is –
Christ. For Christ plays in ten thousand places,
Lovely in limbs, and lovely in eyes not his
To the Father through the features of men's faces.

Herbert's poem addresses directly the relation between Jesus and the sinner which as Pope Francis insists means all of us, especially oneself. The figure of love, the gracious and forgiving host who persists in inviting the 'poet' to a meal which he will serve emerges as the divine saviour of the New Testament, the God who is Love. The poet's continuing protests of his unworthiness as a sinner are finally overcome. So he 'did sit and eat.' This transforming vision of the Eucharist reveals the most intimate companionship between Jesus and the poet, between Jesus and sinners.

Hopkins, one of the language's finest nature poets, invokes another extraordinary vision of Creation and Incarnation to make explicit the encounter between the natural world as captured in beautiful human language, and the presence of the incarnate God, of the Christ at play in 'ten thousand places / ...To the Father through the features of men's faces'. Hopkins may be the most powerful of the near mystic nature poets in the English language and one of the surest poetic guides we have to Jesus' presence to us in creation, both divine and human.

CONCLUSION

The limitations of any attempt to deal with the topic of 'Jesus and Poetry' become more obvious to writer and reader as the work progresses. Some of these have been mentioned already and others must be self-evident. The only one worth mentioning despite its obviousness is the language / geographical restriction, and that only to refer to a serious alternative study which spans continents, civilisations and centuries, by Peggy Rosenthal. Her *The Poets' Jesus*, published by Oxford University Press in

2000, spans the millennia and a range of languages and civilisations beyond the competence of most, but as presented in translation and reflected on is an enormous source for anyone seriously interested in the topic.

A very different but enriching approach might be developed under the rubric 'Jesus as Poet, Jesus as Poem'. But that is a task for another time.

Gwyneth Lewis

FRUIT

Sapling bears a single fruit –
Pomegranate, which I steal

And place it, like a hand grenade,
To ripen on my window sill. I slit

The skin. Its reptile eye
Regards me. Feel the weight,

Its early Dutch Renaissance breast
On which, like Christ the child, I feed,

My mouth its perfect match. Inside's
A honeycomb of ruby rooms

Replete with light. I gorge –
So many mansions! Turn it

Back to fruit (it's toothpick time)
The truth? I'm never the solution.

Thomas McCarthy

IT WAS NOT OUR FAULT

Italy was God's best shot, light of Christ
That shone through Murano glass; a flat
Earth where the heavy velvet calmed each
Argument and indiscretion. God in defeat
Will never again have such assembled
Gold, nor His royal messengers such braid.
Never again will angels have such models
To work upon, such divine perfection
Of youth bred to anchovy and olive grove.

Olives borne down upon Celtic gold,
Mists of faith from a second pressing
Eased the ache of limbs that were pagan:
The good shepherd found a new fold
In a windswept, pig-sticking haven.
It was not our fault that we weren't Italian,
That a sanguine ease never took hold
Among bitter islanders and heathen
Watchers of the treacherous, unsteady sky:

Instead, a wild, divisive Christ
Came in contending fleets from the sea;
Christ as the heir to the Spanish throne
Or Mary, His Mother, as a Scottish queen.
Christ left us wild in the English tongue,
Wild and wandering. It pains me
To see us wandering still, rudderless
In an old Celtic realm, God's lost children –
What a yearning Rome caused within.

Steve Ely

DISMAS THE GOOD THIEF

Compassion, fear of Judgment,
acknowledgment of transgression, acceptance
of earthly justice, implicit repentance,
faith. All in four verses. Christ himself
gave absolution, and why wouldn't he?
He ticked all the boxes. The nails still drove in,
and they had to, being the just sentence
for his crimes; the alternative being
social work and poor-you counselling
from the Howard League for Penal Reform.
But for the serial thefts from ASDA
and Weavers, the Allied Supplies break-ins,
the gang-assaults, arsons, recreation ground rapes:
today shalt thou be with me in Paradise.

Fred Marchant

BEIT SAHUR

– Occupy Boston, December 9, 2011

Black plastic garbage bags flapping away,
 the wind said to be high tonight, half the spaces
  without tents and tarps, some naked ground,
a rain-soft dirt underfoot, the rest just the dull
 paving stones of Dewey Square, all the colours
  muted, as quiet as the few who are left, those
who have decided to be arrested. Stacking,
 packing up the camp library, the kitchen gear,
  counting. Here in the meditation tent someone
is just taking a nap, his legs straight out, kicking
 as if in a bad dream, perhaps, of the sheer glass
  walls I passed on my way, the higher offices,
the brick parapets and vertical cities, the *banca*,
 the lender's tables and their shirted servants
  at the windows looking down over the police
in lime-green dayglo vests. An artist with
 a camera project in mind is shooting the shapes
  that tents will take when the frames are pulled
and the nylon billows like a sail in an eager wind.
 There is no fear anywhere, only the sense that this
  first part is over. In a rough-hewn wooden box
from the Sign Tent, bundles of brown cardboard,
 and in magic marker ink, the wit of the many
  birth pains of a language about ends and means,
packed into a wooden trough, under the chiming of
 the South Station Clock, in this Shepherds' Field,
  Beit Sahur, 'place of the night watch', and manger.

Fred Marchant

A DAY LATER

Thus lines of force pass through us leading
to fields and cities, muddy fingers, a tailor's
needle and thread, an invisible line of hope
that slips through your fingers like water,
takes you to a city of narrow, worn paths,
dark stairs, the rotunda loud with pilgrims
and prayer, a beadle's pointed stick leading
them to the tomb, to gold icons, sad faces.
Outside, squatting in a corner, Coptic priests,
by charcoal fire, heat-treasure, as it is winter,
the day short, and a wind has come up from
the desert. A wood-smell from the fibres of
the planet, a fire with little light but a reason
to chant, and smoke that rises like incense.

Fred Marchant

PARASKEVI

In the Greek, a wide open field of readiness, the long
preparation for the Sabbath, labour starting on Friday,
labour like the months of the Virgin waiting for the birth,

the afternoons of warm milky light that poured into
a whitened room, and over a courtyard swept clean,
and through the wooden doors, through the wide open

palm fronds, their arms framing the worn threshold,
and onto the brass where an unlit candle waited.
One could hear the chanting of a prayer that sounded

like the olive leaves that rustled, bending and bowing
in the wind as if they too were trying to listen in,
to hear words that lived without irony, as if doubt

were the terrible secret at the heart, and deep within
the trunk, within the whorls of wood that denoted a life
had been lived, the pain teaching us to be like the deep,

unsatisfied root searching for the water in clay, doubt
out on the farthest limb, in the rock-hard inedible seed,
new fruit heavy, silver-green with hope, the grove laden.

Author's Note: Paraskevi is the Greek name for Friday, or for St Friday, a virgin-martyr in the Orthodox tradition.

Fred Marchant

SIXTY-SIX

Some late for work, some all business
in stride, some picking up trash bags,
others now waking from a night spent
on the Common. Late summer morning
and what comes to me through the faces
is the story of the death of Tarcisius,
patron saint of altar-boys, the Eucharist
clutched in secret, and close to his heart,
an innocuous child weaving his way
through the dangerous streets of Rome,
persecution ongoing. The taunt-filled
youngsters he meets, they know he is
hiding something. Even as they pummel
him with fist-sized stones, he keeps faith,
guards his treasure, right up to the end.
Second grade when I first heard of this,
sweet Sister Valentine's lesson for life,
the secret we each carry and must never
divulge, for our enemies lounge on every
corner, and the believers on the other side
of the city have been worried, wondering
why you are late, and who has nabbed you.

Harry Clifton

A VISION OF HOKKAIDO IN THE RAIN

A Japanese Christian sect believes Christ visited the country in his unrecorded years

It is very quiet here, in the north of Japan,
Where everyone has forsaken me. The street
Is rain-black, drizzled, and it seems to be winter,
Probably late at night. My second coming,

Unannounced, past any civilised hour,
Is still too soon for redemption. Dark before dawn –
The market closed, the basins for live eels
Stacked neatly. One old woman in black

Squatting under the light of a low-watt bulb
Spoons noodles into herself. Do the old, I wonder,
Go as they always went here – to the boneyard
Deep in the mountains, in the inhuman cold,

And die back into their lines of ancestry?
Laughter behind closed doors, through the masking tape
Of broken, bandaged windows, in the geisha parlour –
Canned American laughter on TV.

Perhaps they are sleeping, though, the guiltless women,
With their clients gone, oblivious on *sake*,
Screen still running. Slide them back, the panels –
Earthly paradise! I have foreshadowed it all,

Of course, from the other side of time
Now here I am. A *tuk-tuk* through the small hours
Sheds its wake of sparks in the neighbouring street
(If everyone were suddenly to awaken ...)

And the elephants, asleep in chains
Outside the sawmill, dream of time and motion
Hauling logs. A whiff of stinking hides –
So this is a town that lives off tannery, then,

And entertains itself, like a million others,
Eating, having sex and watching soaps.
And to speak of evil, as the rain drifts down
Past the naked bulbs of the marketplace

Left on all night, is to know redundancy
Under another wisdom, a different kind of law
Than the one that brought me north, so long ago,
In my lost, apocryphal years

Between the carpenter's shop and the death on the cross.
Perhaps no more was needed. Had I stayed
And intermarried, God alone would have known
And everyone could have slept to the end of time.

Wendell Berry

from A TIMBERED CHOIR

Remembering that it happened once,
We cannot turn away the thought,
As we go out, cold, to our barns
Toward the long night's end, that we
Ourselves are living in the world
It happened in when it first happened,
That we ourselves, opening a stall
(A latch thrown open countless times
Before), might find them breathing there,
Foreknown: the Child bedded in straw,
The mother kneeling over Him,
The husband standing in belief
He scarcely can believe, in light
That lights them from no source we see,
An April morning's light, the air
Around them joyful as a choir.
We stand with one hand on the door,
Looking into another world
That is this world, the pale daylight
Coming just as before, our chores
To do, the cattle all awake,
Our own white frozen breath hanging
In front of us; and we are here
As we have never been before,
Sighted as not before, our place
Holy, although we knew it not.

Icon of Christ the Healer
Icon Chapel, Glenstal Abbey, Murroe, Co Limerick
(see page 74)

Evdokiya Plyuschikha – Valentina Zhogova

1 March (14 March in the new calendar) – the day of saint-martyr Evdokiya, often called Evdokiya Plyuschikha, as on that day the warm spring temperatures make the snow flatten and thaw (the Russian verb '*plyuschit*' means 'to flatten'). She was believed to be in charge of the Spring, and to hold the keys to release the spring waters. This day was especially honoured by women.

Easter – Valentina Zhogova

The date of Easter Sunday, celebrating the resurrection of Jesus Christ, is calculated according to the lunisolar calendar, and for this reason is never fixed. Since the time of first Christians it has been a tradition on the Easter day to greet each other with the words 'Christ has risen!' / 'Indeed He has risen!' and to exchange a triple kiss. Also for Easter Sunday a cake called '*kulich*' is baked, and painted eggs are exchanged.

Yury (Egory) – Valentina Zhogova

23 April (6 May in the new calendar) – the day of St George the Victorious called by people Egory (Yury) the Brave. Traditionally on this day the first cattle are sent to pasture, as Egory was believed to be the protector of domestic cattle.

Trinity – Valentina Zhogova

Trinity, or Pentecost, is celebrated on the fiftieth day after Easter Sunday and symbolises the unity of God in three persons: the Father, the Son, and the Holy Spirit. Trinity is also related to summer vegetation, its primary symbol is the birch tree which is used to decorate churches and homes, along with grasses and flowers.

Peter's swings – Valentina Zhogova

The day of apostles Peter and Paul is celebrated by the Church on 29 June (12 July in the new calendar). It was often called *'Petrov Den'* (St Peter's Day) and together with the Day of St John the Baptist (*Ivan Kupala*) was celebrated in one festive cycle. The main entertainment on that day was the swings which were given a magical meaning – the upward swinging was believed to aid the growth of crops. Also the swings were the meeting place for young people ready to get married.

Intercession of Holy Mother – Valentina Zhogova

On 1 October (14 October in the new calendar) the appearance of the Holy Mother before St Andrew the Fool-for-Christ is celebrated, as is the deliverance of Constantinople from the Saracens. This holiday has a number of meanings, relating to the protective role of the Holy Mother who intercedes for people, protecting them from misfortune; to the snow which usually covers the earth on that day marking the transition from autumn to winter; and to the comparison of the veil of the Holy Mother to the head shawl of a married woman – thus the day is celebrated by brides-to-be.

Ekaterina: sleigh-way opener – Valentina Zhogova

24 November (7 December) in the Orthodox calendar is the day of saint-martyr Ekaterina, called Catherine: sleigh-way opener. Young people celebrate the day by riding one-horse open sleighs, with bobsleighs for children. Newly-married couples who had their wedding in the Autumn used to make their first public appearance on this day, as Catherine was also believed to be a protector of marriage.

John Burnside

OFFICIUM

If therefore thou shalt not watch, I will come on thee as a thief, and thou shalt not know what hour I will come upon thee.
– Revelation 3: 3

It comes to us, after a time,
that there's no forever:

chiffchaff in the hedge, a breath of wind,
that wave of longing in the summer grass

for something other
than the world we've seen;

and how we waited years for an event
that couldn't happen:

footprints in the dew
and *adsit nobis*

sudden in our hearts
like summer rain.

Spiritus Sancti: crickets, thistledown,
a wave of longing in the blood-lit dark

for what we are
beyond the things we seem;

and, quiet, like the ceasing of a drum,
this penitence by halves is scant relief,

if somewhere in the house, unheard, unseen,
eternity comes creeping, like a thief.

George Kalogeris

ICONOSTASIS

In a monastery high up in the mountains of Crete,
Not far from a church with a bombed-out roof, I stand
Before an altar that's four-hundred years old,

And wonder how it survived so many invasions.
That's when the monk takes me around the back,
And shows me the jigsaw pattern behind the panels,

Tracing it with his finger while telling me how
The whole thing comes apart, and that each piece
Is small enough to be safely carried away,

As always happens, he says, when there's an invasion.
And as long as the occupation lasts – which could
Mean decades, if not centuries, filled with bloodshed –

Each family's asked to keep one piece of the altar
Hidden away, inside their house, high up
In the mountains of Crete. And once they're finally gone,

Those hordes of infidels and wild crusaders
Who, as the monk is quick to point out, were no more
Barbaric to the Greeks than the Greeks themselves,

The altar is pieced together again. And then,
After all the bloodshed, the people stand before it
And pray to the powers that protected them:

The Virgin's hands, the Dove, the Logos incarnate.
And this is what's known as *iconostasis*: standing
Face to face with the images of God.

It fits together, he says, like a jigsaw puzzle.

George Kalogeris

ATHANASSIOS

As long as the small white bulb in the votive lamp
Still shone when my room got dark, as dark as the night
Outside, it served, for a time, that light, as a night-light.

High up in the corner, where the ikons were.
So all night long, as long as the bulb stayed on,
That pair of Byzantine faces, aglow in my room.

One was the Virgin holding her child, the other
Some prophet in red velvet robes, with a furry beard
And my father's name, in Greek, *Athanássiós*.

That silver lamp, with its looping tea-kettle handle
And polished gleam, might've been the one that steamed
When Aladdin made his wish. (And down from the ceiling

By three brass chains so lightly the lamp still hovers,
Collecting dust – as long as the spiders, as I
Remember, suspend it from longer, gossamer lines).

High up in my childhood bedroom, above those ikons
Whose lamp-lit eyes were never in the dark,
A pale, faintly quivering halo was cast on the ceiling.

If I couldn't sleep, I was told to tell myself stories.
When my father got really sick, and his heart almost stopped,
My mother would pray each night to *Pánagyía* –

Looking urgently up at the gentle woman's face
Looking down at her from inside a dark blue hood.
(Those fervently moving lips, and that wooden ikon

Void of expression). The Christ child was younger than me,
But looked much older. He was sitting on Mary's lap,
With an open book as big as the Yellow Pages

Cradled upon one arm. When I tried to pronounce
My father's name, in Greek, with his other hand
The Christ child kept two fingers pressed to his lips.

Athanássiós, the prophet, was about to speak.

Author's Note: George Kalogeris writes: Although I grew up in a Greek Orthodox household, my parents' belief was centred more in village ritual than in church doctrine and official ceremony. On the mornings of sacred days my father would bless the house with a basil leaf dipped in holy water before we woke, though sometimes I'd get up in time to see him going from room to room, with the scent still lingering in the hall. My mother never referred to the Holy Virgin by her sovereign, Byzantine appellation of 'Theotokos', but would pray to her using her vernacular name, and usually in the diminutive form, 'Panagyitssa'. When I read Hardy's great poem 'During Wind and Rain' I saw the candles 'mooning each face' as we drove home from midnight service on Easter Saturday, anxious to keep the candles lit so the Sign of the Cross could be made over the threshold of our front door.

Andrew Lansdown

SEHNSUCHT

Everyone else is asleep
and I am up this early
only to keep my small son from crying.

I carry him down to the river.
A slight mist lingers by the bend.
Trees stand on their heads in the still water.

Has he seen a river before?
I can't remember.
He raises his hand,

reaching for it.
He looks back at me
to make sure I have seen it.

How can anyone find anything so amazing?
Yet it's not just the river:
stones, leaves, chickens, fire –

things I still love
though they've fallen familiar –
fill him continually with joy and wonder.

Oo! Oo! he says
as if it hurts him
here in my arms, seeing the river

for the first time.
And a familiar strangeness
grips my heart

and I sing to him
Jesus loves the little children
to keep from weeping.

Andrew Lansdown

MEASURE

I wonder often
these days how much I am loved.
I am well aware
for some the answer's, 'Not much!'
Yet is there nowhere
someone who can say how much?
At the cross, Jesus
himself stretches his free hand
to the nailing place.
He seems to gesture, 'This much!'
But a doubt undoes
my judgment of the measure …
Perhaps he means, 'More than this!'

PATH

If we look we see
the Son's light like the sun's light
makes a straight path
across the sea to each of us
wherever we stand on the shore.

Andrew Lansdown

MAN OF SORROWS

Not so that you would notice –
unless, like me, you were sitting beside him –
my father is weeping. He has removed
his glasses and is dabbing his eyes.
We are singing a hymn – one thousand Christians
singing to our Saviour. But my father
is weeping. What grief has gripped his heart?
His mortality? His two sons who are dead?
The disunity in the Church or the dishonour
in the nation? Perhaps it is just
the unspeakable loneliness of righteousness.
Yes, this most of all. I dare not look at him
lest I, too, should weep. Certainly, Christ
is our Comforter. And He needs to be, too,
being, as He is, the chief cause of our sorrow.

John Ennis

GOING BACK FOR ALL I'D ON

for a plain and ordinary man

I wouldn't mind, it was of the whitest sindon
All of a linen piece what I put on
The best only for such times. Easy for divesting out of,
Brushing against his breast. Where I rested on his love
Beating in my ear. As I'd do nightly. Just another happy supper
So we thought, not sensing the catastrophe,
And we'd never see Yeshua again only altered
Metal through his forearms and his ankles,
Spear hoked deep in his innards beside me now ...

...Creep back with dawn to Gethsemane. The Temple *Who's Who*
Jeering in the courtyard at the purple of his scourging. But not
A trace of it could I find amid the budding olives. In my pelt – I bet
The two soldiers who made a grab for me with their guffawing fists,
A handsome lad to grace them on their rude divan, made off with it.

*

Boanerges no more, that game teenage *son of thunder*
He nicknamed me for I was fearless in our love, het up
Raining blue brimstone on those rejecting him.
Rather, sobered of a sudden, older, I limp
To where I hear the hammers hammering
On some hill like any day round Jerusalem.
But the man they're busy into nailing today
He's not, we reckoned, just one more wannabe messiah.
I can see his pale nakedness tuft through the armoured knee-caps
Of the Romans as they nail and nail into him. Then he's hoisted up.
I climb to stand beside him with his sisters for all the good times
  that have been.
Peter, other males, like the shit they are, are nowhere to be seen.
But there's no hope I can share his pain
Rest my head ever on his breast again ...

*

... In the mid-melée, I hightail it in Gethsemane
Run, dash my foot right bad against a stone:
My left ankle's swollen rotten, starts to stain
Lilac like the flesh on his back with the blows:

God, I'd hoped too he'd have the sense to split
Just as he escaped, gave the hypocrites the slip
Preaching in Nazareth into grim orthodox faces
The pure shite they were, who in a fury rushed
Us in the small, tight-arsed, low-ceilinged synagogue:
Jostling to whom the honour to dash his brains out on the rocks
over the cliff edge
Yelling *bastard, bastard*. Should have done that, they pant after, at his birth.
Our eyes meet again under the rising sun up in the heavens.
I keep praying for that miracle. That a couple of angels
Descend, undo him from the tree, but they never do.

*

His eyes redden to me *mind her for me will you*
As they roll in his sockets sunk with the agony,
Slew to where his mother stands with his Magdala
Partner, who's got a profession to feed the kid on;
But the mother, who trails his lakes and parables,
She'll gather no more the morsels from his tables
To feed the stray hungry dogs that wag their tails.
I see him a boy immersed back in her tenderness.
Pain rattles him so bad it's into a spearing numbness.
I've to think on my feet of her when I'd keen on unashamed:
What to do when all this bother's a memory, and his brother James
Is butchered, where to head for, lead that stout woman by the hand
Out of moonlit Jerusalem. Romans break jittery doors for us at dawn,
Weeping in our faces all year till we wash, pack away his bones ...

*

But he strides right back among us, Yeshua, as he promises.
Think I'm one of the first to hear him with my own ears
Singing in the whirlwind with any smash of thunder
Remonstrating in my skull. Walk the walk, the burning bush

Of morning's ferocious sunlight in the sepulchre.
Can't stop the talking about it and am talking still
As you see dust gather on the cups in Ephesus.
The hand that keeps our house these happy decades
Does not slip in and out of mine any more.
Mary has died. No cups for two anymore.
And her vulva that opens among the cattle
As he slides out in the liquids of her body,
Her going is in Bethlehem just like today.

*

Nothing sadder than two Sadduccees peering
Into empty wine jars and they fasting for this for weeks.
Nothing sadder than a groom sensing disaster
And the story in people's mouths till he'd die.
Nothing sadder than a steward with his authority deflated.
Nothing sadder than guests on camels from a distance
Rising to yoke up for the nearest watering hole.
Nothing sadder than a bride facing this miscarriage.
Nothing sadder than I do not get the time
To write the books about him I want to,
The stories she tells me of her Yeshua
As boy, teenager, in his early twenties:
Bread. Bread. Always Bread. The night's on us,
And Mary cold at Ephesus.

*

And how the vested, and vestmented, interests howl
Like jackals in the night of their worst nightmare.
The hour's at hand with bones ossaried with initials
His, his partner's, their kid before the scatter comes.
Yes, you've a right to howl, you jackals that lose little time
Out-templing temples even those of far Rome, sad, sublime
Babels when all we need, any of us, is a table or two in a room.
House. Shed. A safe flat rock like in bad times with bread and wine.
Speak the words into his blood-red wine, God, the good stuff, keep it
  pouring   pouring   pouring
For the brother in Cana, when just one amid the seventy-two, I gate crash

His dance with Mary from over Magdala. The mother cornering the two *they have no wine*
He flushed from it, dancing a *karar*, backanswers *what is that to me*
Stories told of the wine jars, I hear they drink from them still.

Daniel Tobin

MOUNT OF OLIVES

Via Dolorosa, the grief-stricken road,
  a sun-dashed scar through the city's sacred heart,
all flaring shadow and gritted light unending
  on stones where you walked, loving your enemies.

A sun-dashed scar through the city's sacred heart
  ran through yours, blood-battered like your journey
on stones where you walked, loving your enemies,
  their stark unknowing, you bearing the blunt weight.

It ran through you, blood, battered on its journey
  from black hole through plasma cloud over light years
unknowing, everything bearing its own blunt weight
  then blinking out, alone, though growing wakeful

from black hole through plasma cloud over light years
  Micron by micron, in the full reach of you
unblinking, alone, you groaning and wakeful
  to worm and scavenger and a hill of skulls.

Micron by micron, in the full reach of you,
  is that not where the circuit leads, or nothing,
only worm and scavenger, a stark hill of skulls
  vaster than expanding space, its dark matter

the Not where your sad circuit leads, each nothing
  flashing past, the flesh felt, inveterate earth
an asterisk of expanding space, the Nothing *mattered*,
  your body naked, nailed, a face on a rag?

This felt flesh flashing past, inveterate earth,
  is past, through you in you, all ends surpassing,
while the bodies, naked, nailed, sad faces on rags,
  turn shimmers of leaves on the Mount of Olives,

in you all ends surpassed, through you this last passing
  like the pressed, virgin fruit of ancient trees,
leaves brightened by wind along the Mount of Olives
  above the grief-stricken road, Via Dolorosa –

all sun-dashed where we walk in the light unending.

Sujata Bhatt

FLORENCE

He sent her a postcard from Florence –
a view of the city, his own photograph, actually –
chosen with care. He couldn't help it,
the words just came to his lips,
and he said them aloud as he wrote
for my love, noli me tangere –

That's when she decided to end it.
After all, who did he think he was? Jesus?
And what did he mean
by *for my love*? I love you, but
let me go my way – and you, go yours.

Afterwards, he could never explain it.
He told her it was the scent of oranges
that had confused him –
and he had been distracted by the sparrows.
How he had watched a male sparrow feed
his fledglings, those fluffy, quivering feathery beings,
fat and floppy, not at all ready to fly.
They were so helpless in the courtyard
where he sat writing – but he felt more helpless
that day, and he felt one particular fledgling's open beak
was his own soul wanting more, something more –
he didn't know what. Then, he told her it was the sky
at night, the stars – constellations he wanted to follow
and so he hardly closed his eyes.
It was the moon, he said, that kept him awake
and confused – And then mornings, the sun
always too bright – all day –
He started to miss clouds, he said, softer shadows –

Afterwards, he told her it was a mistake –
he meant to say: *marry me, please* –

Silent all this time, she merely smiled –
such quietness and clarity in her face.
There was a strange sweetness in the air –

bruised pears – lilies gaping by the window –
and they could hear the neighbour's son
struggling with his cello –
What was she thinking?
As always, he didn't know.

Then, she gave him back his words
    noli me tangere –
spoken so softly
as if she meant the opposite –
and then she left.

Sujata Bhatt

VIRIDITAS: HILDEGARD AND JESUS

She follows the cries of birds.

She moves as if she has just stepped out of a song.

Yes – and she is the song itself
before it had ever been sung –
before it had lived within anyone's breath –

*

Let us not diminish her power,
let her words live the way she meant them –
But keep her human, keep her contradictions.

Restore the metaphors, restore the Mysteries –
but also
restore the human heart within the human body.

*

And Hildegard, a virgin, knew how love
burns through us – how it hungers –
a flower whose roots can suck everything out of our souls –
and she imagined the pleasure of skin on skin –
of blood and muscle – Some call her fearless –
She knew herself as an instrument of God.

*

The journey was long and it had rained
for weeks – greenness seeped back into the earth –

The birds were many and loud.

Her world was not innocent –
but the forests had not been tamed, the animals
had not been driven out and killed.

There were flowers we will never see,
birds we will never hear –

Nights were darker then, silver-veined with rivers,
rivers glinting with the eyes of fish
as starlight flashed through the current –
Nights the rivers pulsed with trembling gills,
water streaming, rushing against so many thrashing tails –

She would have heard wolves calling –
She would have known where bears foraged –

She, who was no longer young,
walked for months, for years through this landscape –

*

This time,
when she arrived, the people were there, waiting for her –
anxious, desperate – huddled together
in their small chapel. She could smell the sickness
on their breath – their faces scarred
and discoloured from so many ailments –
The warmth they brought, fetid with fever.

*

Die Seele durchfließt den Leib
  wie der Saft den Baum.

And if the soul flows through the body,
the way sap flows through the tree –
then, does blood flow also through the soul?

Where does the body end and the soul begin?

And will the soul itself, the pure soul,
heal the blood, heal the body?

*

I have never seen you so hungry, my Lord –

This is what I hear her say, over and over again –

Whatever I say, you will know
whether it is the Truth or not –
so why should I hide, why pretend?

This time, when I stepped forward
to address the people, I could not speak,
I did not know what to say –
words failed me. I looked down at my hands
and wished myself back in my garden –
When I looked up, you were there –
I had not seen you enter.

I knew it was you, Jesus, my Lord,
even though you tried to pretend
you were someone else, an ordinary man,
or at most an angel, Michael perhaps,
but without a sword. And I understood
   that only I could see you.

You were enclosed within a pale, golden light –
brighter than the morning sun
            falling across fresh snow –
and you were the source of this flickering brilliance.
Your face, rosy – not gaunt anymore –
And then I saw the basket at your feet.
You told me to speak – 'Whatever you say
will be fine,' you gestured – 'say whatever
you think, whatever you want to say.'

And then, you started to eat –
one fish after another, you pulled out
from your basket. I have never seen you
so hungry, my Lord, so famished –
as if no one had ever nurtured you.
You simply ate and ate, the soft meat still firm,
now a splayed glistening in your hands –
how you tore the white flesh with your teeth
as I started to speak. I have never seen you like this,

my Lord, as if you meant to return
to earth for good, as if you wanted to be
human again, mortal again –

I have never seen you so hungry, my Lord –

Author's Note: 'Hildegard' refers, of course, to Hildegard von Bingen (1098-1179). There is one quotation: the lines in German are from her work, *Scivias*, originally written in Latin.

John Poch

GOOD GOD

They ate of the tree of knowledge, then they fell
toward labour, labour, and the existential.
The good I want I do not do, as well.

And worse, I do the same old raising hell,
and repetition loves the consequential.
They ate of the tree of knowledge, then they fell.

For this then that: I sob in each blood cell.
I aim to love but wax self-referential.
The good I want I do not do as, well,

gracefully as a swell-tossed buoy bell.
The fruitless floats and calls with dark potential.
They ate of the tree of knowledge, then we fell

for it, the lie and the fact we most retell
because we need to get at the essential
The Good. I want. I do not do as well

as Eve. It's me, St Paul, but not my fall.
Come, second Adam, mercy exponential,
for they ate of the tree of knowledge, then they fell,
and the good I want I do not do, as well.

John Poch

MINE

Hungry, you call me by your name. Under
barbed wire and up arroyos I come crawling,
crowbarring old boards from your mouth and wonder.
I have the ancient map, a torch, a calling

to disinter a treasure. At the surface,
before I take my last white breath, I call
in like a bat relinquishing its purchase.
I follow hunger's swallow, my fortunate fall

through black to gold, my narrow way through myriad
prospects of living in the world, when
(save for one ascended) even the buried
and resurrected man must die again.

From darkness, you call me yours, for words, worth earth.
You call me in: Lazarus come forth.

Gillian Allnutt

IGNOMINY

Withal I know the lovely lone laboriousness of being

like cloud in the making.

I stand, alone, mistaken

in undress.

The crows erupt, like words, around me –

Lord, Lord –

with all their raucousness.

TO GOD MY GOD

Let me in You alone have leave to steer

not by the loud and tawdry, by the light fantastic of the hour

but, unawed, constellated, by the less familiar love and fear.

Gillian Allnutt

'IT IS SNOWING'

it is snowing

on earth

in the heart

bird-hunger

that of

the linnet

flown

to iberia

Gillian Allnutt

'AS IT WERE HUNGER'

as it were hunger

happen

in my heart

as it were hunger

happen

in the king whose bare ship burial

in the pauper, then, whose kepier hospital

as I were one

in whom the hunger of the lord

might be laid down

a while a while and *yet a little while*

as it were hoard

Notes
Kepier Hospital: an almshouse founded in Durham in the twelfth century.
yet a little while: words of Jesus spoken at John 7:33 and in several other places in that Gospel.

Mark Patrick Hederman

BEES OF THE INVISIBLE

I do not remember a time in my life when I was not aware of God's presence as a definite reality but without specific contours. If I were to put a finger on it now it would be something like fog clouds, or air, and more especially, wind.

At a positive level this meant that my relationship with the entire world around me was permeated by this presence. It was a pervasive atmosphere. I was in love with the world in a way that can be described as universal. God's presence radiating outwards from the breathing heart embraces the whole world before returning like rain or like dew on the grass all around. It is in this sense that I call myself 'Catholic,' the Greek word for 'universal'. I identify with the whole world in this way.

At a negative level this presence was irritating, like clouds of midges on a summer day. As if I was being stalked by someone I never actually saw, but whose scent lingered in the atmosphere.

I have been haunted by God's presence all my life. I can only describe it as a timid and painfully sensitive aristocrat who disappears when the slightest movement is made in his or her direction; who waits and watches with tremulous delight and eager attention at the other side of a hedge. Any attempt to acknowledge this presence makes it start and disappear. Anxiously friendly, curiously terrified, like wild deer in a wood, God has a horror of imposing, or becoming unbearable. And yet, there is this helpless almost pathetic plea for acknowledgement, nothing more than an understated gesture, a signal through the absent prevalence.

Awareness of this obsession, the contact which eventually builds up, in my case for sixty years now, proves to be enduring, rewarding, worthwhile, even though always conducted at God's tempo, in God's idiom, with almost painful minimalism and self-restraint. Eventually I make the psalm my own: 'One thing I ask of the Lord, for this I long; to dwell in the house of the Lord all the days of my life.'

I am one of God's secret agents in the world, reluctant, disloyal, unfit for purpose. So many bumbling, cowardly, pathetic right-hand men come to mind: Sancho Panza, Manuel of *Fawlty Towers*, Captain Boyle's friend, Joxer Daly, Falstaff. And yet, without other more reliable allies, God sends flocks of angels to help me out, prevent me from making irreparable mistakes. These fussily guide me along the right path, without altogether breaching conventions about free will. Their annoying presence resembles the cortège trying to prevent the Rape of Belinda's lock of hair in Alexander Pope's ludicrously distraught sit-com:

But when to Mischief Mortals bend their Will,
How soon they find fit Instruments of Ill!
Just then, Clarissa drew with tempting Grace
A two-edg'd Weapon from her shining Case;
So Ladies in Romance assist their Knight,
Present the Spear, and arm him for the Fight.
He takes the Gift with rev'rence, and extends
The little Engine on his Finger's Ends:
This just behind Belinda's Neck he spread,
As o'er the fragrant Steams she bends her Head:
Swift to the Lock a thousand Sprights repair,
A thousand Wings, by turns, blow back the Hair,
And thrice they twitch'd the Diamond in her Ear,
Thrice she look'd back, and thrice the Foe drew near.

– 'THE RAPE OF THE LOCK', CANTO III

The icon of Christ the Healer has been my constant companion for over forty years. It is a simple composition with Jesus facing the viewer. He wears a silvery garment and there is a white nimbus around his head. He is blessing with his right hand and holding open the Gospel book with his left hand pointing to the text from Matthew, 11: 28-30: 'Come to me all you who are weary and carry heavy burdens and I will give you rest.' The colouring is autumnal: browns and yellows in deepening shades, but the brightening yellow around the figure gives the feeling of fire, and the warmth of a hearth. This icon and its companions belonged to White Russians exiled in the 1920s after the Russian revolution. The icons were bought in Paris and were given to the monastery at Glenstal Abbey in the 1950s by the Grattan-Esmonde family. At the time the icons were not really appreciated by the Glenstal community who found them somewhat alien as religious art. Many of us had special favourites which we commandeered. I was moved by this icon and I hung it in my bedroom from the early 1970s to April 1988 when it was placed on the arch into the right aisle of the icon chapel at Glenstal Abbey. Since then I visit it at least once a day and allow its gentle compassionate face to gaze into mine. I travel through the deep vertiginous eyes to the place beyond them where Christ is, at this moment and at every moment, at the right hand of the Father in the presence of the Holy Spirit. Making that connection takes me to their space which is the nearest I get, in this present life, to being in the place prepared for me since the beginning of time. The icon acts as a sacramental which makes the connection between me and the Holy Trinity each time I stand in its presence. It is not in any way that I worship it or mistake it for what it represents; it provides a setting and a focus which allow me to unlock the barrier to another world where the presence of Christ is living and reigning forever and ever. I am grateful to this icon for seeking me out.

How do we establish a way of life here on earth which will allow us to be in constant connection with the three persons of the Trinity? Monastic life is one way of doing this. We construct a spaceship which straddles two worlds without losing touch with either: here and now, eternity and infinity, two kinds of space and two kinds of time.

Benedict of Nursia who lived in the fifth century left a blueprint, a handbook, for such a machine and some of us have been using his technology ever since. No one can understand our life as monks unless they recognise that our primary work is holding open four times a day, every day of the week, every week of the year, a space where God can be present in our world.

Here is an image of what a monk might be, borrowed from the world of insects: fire ants from the rainforests of Brazil. Finding themselves 'thrown,' in a very postmodern way, into a particularly rain-drenched area of the world, these tiny creatures build rafts – made up of themselves. They connect by gripping each others' mandibles and claws as we might lock shoulders together, to weave a waterproof fabric. Mandibles, by the way, are appendages near the mouth which were originally designed to grasp, crush, or cut food, or to defend against predators and rivals. Such weapons of mass destruction are turned into communitarian safety belts in the interests of survival. One half of these ants cling together underneath in a single layer – the others form a chain mail covering on top. The resulting two-tiered raft is cohesive, buoyant and water-repellent. The ants below survive because the hairs on their bodies are designed to trap small pockets of air which prevent them from drowning.

Monks overcome their propensity to drown in a chaotic world, by forming such a choir. Their circle is constituted through the psalms they sing and the air they breathe. Our 'chorus'(a Greek word for a different kind of theatrical space between two worlds) creates a platform between this world and the world beyond. This human circle provides the opening through which the Holy Spirit can breathe into this world. Monks are guardians of this source of oxygen. Our breathing in and out in song is confined-space ventilation ducting. Through such prayer, the breath of the Holy Spirit can catch itself on the sprockets of exhalation and secrete itself into the emerging world. That is our role in the new creation of that world. We are a singing people defined by our song. Song is our existence. Our liturgy 'enacts a world where the hinted possibilities whispered by the Spirit can be given consideration'[1], can become flight-paths in an ever expanding runway. We sing the song of a world open to such possibility. The liturgy produces honey from the rocks, from the secret places of the earth. We are bees of the invisible who, through this liturgical work, make visible and palpable the reality, the presence of the other world, which manifests itself through our ritual in a luminosity or phosphorescence.

We, as human beings, alone of all the inhabitants of the earth are capable of praise. Our task, as human beings, is to achieve the balance between the gravity of the earth and the openness to the Spirit: the space between 'the within and the without'. To live the 'outside', to allow its breath to seep up through us so that we become its sound-box – this is what the earth is asking of us.

> Yes the springtime did need you.
> Many stars demanded
> that you sense them. A wave
> long since gone by lifted itself toward you,
> or when you passed a window that was open, a violin
> gave itself up. All this was charge.
> But did you complete it?
>
> Earth, is it not this that you want: invisibly
> to arise in us? Is it not your dream
> to become one day invisible? – Earth! Invisible!
> What do you charge us with if not transformation?
> Earth, my love, I will. Oh believe me,
> Further springtimes are
> not required to win me –
> On my word, a single one, a single May
> is too much for my blood.
> I have been your
> tongue-tied subject
> for far too many years.
>
> – RAINER MARIA RILKE, 'FIRST DUINO ELEGY'

Each one of us in the monastery gives our self to such co-operative world-construction as one silken thread that believes in the beauty of the whole tapestry or carpet.

> Avoid the illusion that there can be any lack
> for someone who wishes, then fully decides: to be!
> Silken thread, you were woven into the fabric.
>
> Whatever the design with which you are inwardly joined
> (even for only one moment amid years of grief),
> feel that the whole, the marvellous carpet is meant.
>
> – RAINER MARIA RILKE, *SONNETS TO ORPHEUS*

As an anonymous community who gather in the church four times a day, we are thinning the air of pure human purpose so that the will of God, and thereby 'the kingdom of God', can enter in. 'O gates, lift high your heads, grow higher ancient doors, let him enter the King of Glory!'

To achieve this purpose we have to empty our hearts and lay them out like the petals of a rose which 'sleeps under manifold lids.'[2] There is no signature to this tune. We have to evacuate our egos and turn them into segments of a larger reality. This dethronement of the ego and abdication of our sovereign wills in favour of the container we create by such self-emptying, is the way in which the incarnation of God can be continued and extended into the contemporary world, so that we too become the body of Christ. And it has to be done as a community. No one can perform a liturgy on their own. It is not the work of an individual. Each one of us has to give ourselves to the work as a silken thread that believes in the beauty of the carpet. Every time I look around me in choir I am gratified and amazed to see twenty others engaged in this work consistently and dutifully.

Wallace Stevens reminds us: 'It is certain that the experience of the poet is of no less a degree than the experience of the mystic and we may be certain that in the case of the poets, the peers of the saints, these experiences are of no less a degree than the experiences of the saints themselves.'[3]

This is why Rainer Maria Rilke's poetry is an important expression of religious practice. As Rilke himself writes in a letter:[4]

> It can hardly be said to what degree a human being can carry himself over into an artistic concentration as dense as that of the Elegies and certain sonnets; often it is uncanny for the person who brought them forth to feel beside him, on the thinner days of life (the many!), such an essence of his own being, in its indescribable, ultimate weight. The presence of a poem like this stands out, in the strangest way, above the flatness and insignificance of daily life, and yet precisely out of that daily life was this greater, more valid existence wrested and achieved (how, the achiever himself hardly knows); for hardly has it been done before one again belongs in the general, blinder fate, among those who forget, or know as if they didn't know, and who through an easy vagueness or inexactness help increase the sum of life's mistakes. In this way, every great artistic achievement, even to its furthest possible success, is both a distinction and a humiliation for the one who was capable of it.

Our community at prayer provides a landing-strip for the Holy Spirit. Our new being together is beyond ontology, stretching towards infinity, in a company of doxology: praise – thanksgiving – as a way of being – a stance – a posture – which uses the liturgy as a trellis or as a brace, a support system, to maintain this co-operative presence. 'Praise is about an inner marriage. And an outer one – us and the world. Somehow we are harmonizing with the world.'[5] Walter Bruegemann has identified and nominated the particular stance, the precise posture, the prevailing attitude which marks liturgical co-creation. He calls it 'doxology,' the 'right way' to give praise to God. Doxology, or the liturgy of 'praise,' is not a response to a world already fixed and settled, it is participation in a world in process of being decreed through this liturgical act. Liturgy is a cloth of gold, a many-splendoured dream coat, woven like a cobweb between the fingertips of the human and the divine. Any socialism unable to accommodate both God and humankind is a socialism too narrow for us.

> Silent friend of many distances, feel
> how your breath enlarges all of space.
> Let your presence ring out like a bell
> into the night. What feeds upon your face
>
> grows mighty from the nourishment thus offered.
> Move through transformation, out and in.
> What is the deepest loss that you have suffered?
> If drinking is bitter, change yourself to wine.
>
> In this immeasurable darkness, be the power
> that rounds your senses in their magic ring,
> the sense of their mysterious encounter.
>
> And if the earthly no longer knows your name,
> whisper to the silent earth: I'm flowing.
> To the flashing water say: I am.[6]
>
> — *SONNETS TO ORPHEUS*

The question is how do we keep this possibility open at all times and the answer to this question is that we try to live liturgically which means that we embed into the time/space structure of our lives a scaffolding which undergirds the everyday and allows it to be permeated with breath from elsewhere. We have to learn the rhythm, the tempo and the meaning of this breath. We learn a new language. We compare our efforts to the 'miracle' which occurred in Tuscumbia in Alabama in 1887. Anne Sullivan taught Helen Keller who was blind, deaf and dumb, how to finger spell. Helen had until that moment not yet fully understood the meaning of words. She led her to the water pump on 5 April 1887. As Anne pumped the water over Helen's hand, Anne spelled out the word 'water' in the girl's free hand. Something about this explained the meaning of words within Helen, and Anne could immediately see in her face that she finally understood.

> We have overheard fountains all our days.
> They sound to us almost like time.
> But so much more closely do they keep pace
> with eternity's subtle rhythm.[7]
>
> — *SONNETS TO ORPHEUS*

And this work of liturgical prayer is not just teaching those who partake the meaning of words and things, it is also transforming the things themselves. Rilke, as a poet, recognises that he can rescue objects from time by transforming them within, and expressing them in song. He discovers, through his poetic art, the ability to transform consciousness and world by having them interact in the poetic image.[8] In other words, his task is also a liturgical consecration. His poetry becomes one of praise and transformation. In the *Sonnets to Orpheus*, Rilke takes Orpheus as the archetype of the inspired singer and the founder of all mystery religions, the first to reveal to us the meaning of initiation rites. Living like Orpheus – or living the *Orphikos bios* (the Orphic way of life) – means living the liturgical life of the greatest musician and poet of Greek myth. 'Ultimately there is only one poet, that infinite one who makes himself felt, here and there through the ages, in a mind that can surrender to him.'[9] When we reach the depth of singing we are no longer ourselves; we become Orpheus, the one and only singer who is The Holy Spirit. 'By the end of the book', Mitchell tells us in his introduction to the sonnets, 'Rilke is no longer addressing Orpheus. He has become Orpheus, and can speak to his personal self from the centre of the universe. The cycle is completed. Life resolves in a single breath, and the tree of song that sprang up in the first line of the first sonnet is transformed into the serene, rooted "I am" that is the Sonnets' last word, the word uttered at every moment by each particular form, and also the name of God.'[10]

> And where there had been
> At most a makeshift hut to receive the music,
>
> a shelter nailed up out of their darkest longing
> with an entryway that shuddered in the wind –
> you built a temple deep inside their hearing.
>
> — *SONNETS TO ORPHEUS*

This temple built inside our hearing is the liturgy of the hours as we sing it every day of our lives. And Orpheus is both Christ and the Holy Spirit, the song of the interior fountain that wells up in our hearts.

> And it was almost a girl and came to be
> out of this single joy of song and lyre ...
> and made herself a bed inside my ear.
>
> — *SONNETS TO ORPHEUS*

> A god can do it. But will you tell me how
> a man can enter through the lyre's strings?
> Our mind is split.
>
> Simple, for a God.
> But when can we be real?
> Young man,
> forget your own passionate loving and music ...
> True singing is a different breath, about
> nothing. A gust inside the god. A wind.
>
> — *SONNETS TO ORPHEUS*

Monks have to renounce their own passionate love songs, their own vocation to be poets, and take up the task of mediating another kind of sound:

> For it is the god. His metamorphosis
> in this and that ...
>
> It is Orpheus once for all
> whenever there is song.

This other kind of singing stems from one original and ultimate source which has now become twofold. Since the incarnation there is a double world and Christ is part of both, as we can also be, if we join this singing from the other world.

When Eurydice, the wife of Orpheus, died from a serpent's bite, he went down into the underworld to bring her back. His songs were so beautiful that Hades agreed to let her go back to earth. The music of Orpheus could tame wild beasts and make rocks and trees move to his rhythm. Whenever we reach a certain depth with music that carries our praise and thanksgiving to ultimate depths, then it is always Orpheus who sings: 'It is Orpheus once for all wherever there is song.'

Rilke's Sonnet 7, Part One, is the most precise and vivid description of our song:

Praising is what matters! He was summoned for that,
and came to us like the ore from a stone's
silence. His mortal heart presses out
a deathless, inexhaustible wine.

Whenever he feels the god's paradigm grip
his throat, the voice does not die in his mouth.
All becomes vineyard, all becomes grape,
ripened on the hills of his sensuous south.

Neither decay in the sepulchre of kings
nor any shadow fallen from the gods
can ever detract from his glorious praising.

For he is a herald who is with us always,
holding far into the doors of the dead
a bowl with ripe fruit worthy of praise.

Most people who explain the liturgy try to picture for us what happens at the other side of the tapestry where Christ sits in glory at the right hand of the Father in the eternal heavenly worship of the Trinity, surrounded by choirs of angels and saints. But we who are still on this earth have no real capacity to understand or appreciate what happens in this other dimension. We are desperately extending our human and earthly tendrils, hoping to find some meaningful, sensuous, emotional, psychological and human pitons[11] which we can grasp and hang on to as we climb this wall between ourselves and eternity. Because it is a wall and there will always be a wall between us and what lies ahead or beyond our human lives. The wall is both a separation and a means of communication between the two.

Christ has unearthed this wall and covered it with his fingerprints so that we can identify his handiwork. Liturgy is both a barrier and a 'way through' to the 'other' world. The physical world, with everything in it, serves the same purpose as a blind person's stick. Anything here can be used to tap out our relationship with God as blind people tap their way through the world. The stick does not give direct insight but is used to bring us into practical contact with a reality which is otherwise obscured. So, the liturgy is the braille we have devised to allow us, who are blind, deaf and dumb in the world of the Spirit, to achieve contact. 'Jerusalem is built as a city' the psalm tells us. It is an image or a symbol of the place where God can dwell on earth. And we create this city, this place, these walls, by doing liturgy. We have to learn this language and teach it to others. Most people educated in the twenty-first century will be blind and deaf to this language of symbolism. We have sold our birthright for the monochrome, monocultural pottage of science and technology. Science and technology are, of course, very wonderful and world-improving, but they are not everything. Unless we are also introduced to the other language of symbolism, we miss the 'many splendoured thing'; the other side of the coin. Without access to this other dimension, the world we live in is 'a dry weary land without water'. Monks sit and tend the opening to the well.

Notes

1 Walter Brueggemann: *Israel's Praise* (Fortress Press, 1988).

2 Twice in my life I have learned from Rainer Maria Rilke how poetry can describe the life we are trying to live. The *Duino Elegies* describe the balance between two worlds which monastic life tries to achieve. The *Sonnets to Orpheus* describe a life for which song has become existence. Rilke takes Orpheus as the archetype of the inspired singer and the founder of all mystery religions, the first to reveal to us the meaning of initiation rites. Living like Orpheus or living the *Orphikos bios* means living the liturgical life of the greatest musician and poet of Greek myth.

3 Stephen Mitchell gives this quotation in his notes to the sonnets on page 158. It is taken from Wallace Stevens, *The Necessary Angel* (Knopf, 1951).

4 Mitchell's translation, pp. 161-2, from a letter to Countess Mirbach, 9 August 1924.

5 Li-Young Lee, 'The Subject is Silence' in *A God in the House*.

6 Rainer Maria Rilke, *The Sonnets to Orpheus*, Part II, XXIX. I am using the translation with an introduction and notes by Stephen Mitchell (Simon & Schuster, 1985).

7 Ibid. Appendix VIII.

8 *The Cambridge Companion to Rilke*, edited by Karen Leeder and Robert Vilain (Cambridge University Press, 2010).

9 Letter to Narmy Wunderly from Volkart, 29 July 1920, quoted by Stephen Mitchell, op.cit. p. 164.

10 Stephen Mitchell, op. cit. p 10.

11 A piton is a metal spike (usually steel) that is driven into a crack or seam in the rock with a hammer, and which acts as an anchor to protect the climber against the consequences of a fall, or to assist progress.

James Harpur

THE WHITE SILHOUETTE

– for John F Deane

'There went a whisper round the decks one morning, "We have a mysterious passenger on board." … Often I thought of that rumour after we reached Jerusalem … When I saw the man all in white by the Golden Gate carrying in all weather his lighted lamp, I always thought, "There is a mysterious pilgrim in Jerusalem."'

– Stephen Graham, from *With The Russian Pilgrims to Jerusalem* (1913)

I thought we would meet in a holy place
Like the church in the hamlet of Bishopstone
Empty on a Wiltshire summer's day
The trees full of rooks and hung in green
And the stream in the meadows a rush
Of darkling silver beneath the bridge
Where I saw my first kingfisher flash
Its needle, leaving its turquoise stitch
In my memory; and I would sit
In the church and close my eyes
And wait in vain for something to ignite
And wonder whether this was my life
Wasting away in my mother's home.
Sometimes I'd bring Herbert's *Temple*
And read the quiet order of his poems
And picture him, as once he was glimpsed,
Hugging the floor in his church at Bemerton
Asking love to bid him welcome.
I sat with an upright praying disposition
Preoccupied in self-combing
Too callow and spiritually impatient
To notice if you had slipped in
As a tourist to inspect the choir or font
And buy a picture postcard and sign
The book with 'lovely atmosphere';
Or as a walker taking refuge from rain
Or a woman primping flowers by the altar.

Or somewhere like the island of Patmos
Out of season and the tourist flow,
The sea leeching blue from the skies.
In the cave of St John, pointillist gold
On tips of candles and highlights of icons,
You might have visited that day in September
When I was there, absorbing the coolness,
Imagining John on the Day of the Lord
Prostrate on the ground as if before a throne
And you not dressed in a 'robe and gold sash'
Nor with hair 'as white as wool or snow'
But as a pilgrim with camera and rucksack
Respectful, curious, guide-book in hand
Appreciating the grain of raw stone
Catching my eye and pausing for a second
As if I were a schoolfriend from years ago.
I never saw you, if you were there,
For I was too blinded by the new Jerusalem
Flashing out jasper, topaz, sapphire
Descending from heaven like a huge regal crown.

Or somewhere like Holycross in Tipperary,
The abbey at the meeting of road and river,
You might have stopped to break a journey
As I often do, and seen me there in the nave
Ambling down the sloping floor
Towards the relic-splinter of the Cross
Or sitting outside on the banks of the Suir
On a bench on a swathe of tended grass
Perhaps that day when, heading north,
I paused by the car park to watch
A bride, fragile, and frozen by the door
Her bridesmaids huddled in the cold of March
Waiting and waiting to make her entrance
Into the sudden shine of turning faces
Like a swan gliding in its snowdress
From an arch of the bridge in a state of grace.
I was too mesmerised by her destiny
To see you start your car, drive off,
And raise your hand as you passed me by
On the way to Cashel, Fermoy and the South.

But there was that time I was so certain
That I had finally found you;
Sick at home, I turned to meditation
And prayer to overcome self-pity
For weeks accumulating quietude
Till that morning when seconds were emptied out
My thoughts cleansed, my self destroyed
Within an uncanny infusing light
That seemed to deepen and unfold
More layers of radiance and lay me wide open
So you could cross the threshold
Or I could cross, at any moment.
But I closed the door of my heart, afraid,
Who knows, that I might have met you
Afraid I would pass to the other side
And never return to all that I knew;
I thought I could always re-open myself
And greet you properly, well prepared.
I never did. I feared that sudden shift
Into the zone of timelessness; too scared
I looked for you in public, for safety,
I kneeled in churches, gave the sign
Of peace in St James's Piccadilly,
I recited prayers, took bread and wine
And I concentrated so hard, but failed
To believe they were your blood and body;
I heard staccato prayers, like nails
Banged in, as if to board up windows.

Sometimes I'd sense you as a glimmer
As in that dream I once had out of the blue
When you stood at night on a Greek island shore;
Your face was hidden, but it was you;
The stars pinned in place the layers of darkness
Then came the comets, perhaps a dozen,
Their tails fanned out with diminishing sparks;
Slowly they twisted and turned – your hands
Moving in concert, as if you were guiding them,
As if they were on strings, like Chinese kites.
The comets slowed and stopped, and changed
Into letters of Hebrew, emblazoning the night.
And I knew if I could grasp those words,

Your silent message across the stars,
I'd know my destiny on earth.
Instead I woke, as puzzled as Belshazzar.

I do not search for you any more
I don't know whom to seek, or where;
Too weary, disillusioned, I'm not sure
What I think or if I really care
That much; my last hope – that my resignation
Might be a sign of the *Via Negativa*,
A stage of my self-abnegation –
That hope prevents the thing it hopes for.

And yet

I still write to you, poem after poem,
Trying to shape the perfect pattern
Of words and the mystery of their rhythm,
An earthly music audible in heaven –
Each poem is a coloured flare
A distress signal, an outflowing
Of myself, a camouflaged prayer
Dispatched towards the Cloud of Unknowing
And all I have to do is stay
Where I am, ready to be rescued
Not move, speak or think but wait
For the brightening of the Cloud
For your white silhouette to break
Free from it and come nearer, nearer,
Till I see your essence and I can ask
Where in the world you were
Throughout my days – and only then
Will I grasp why I never found you
Because you were too close to home
Because I thought I'd have to die
To see you there, right there, removing
The lineaments of your disguise –
My careworn wrinkled skin
My jaded incarnation of your eyes –
My face becoming your face
My eyes your eyes
I you us   I you us
Iesus.

Robert Cording

ADVENT STANZAS

I.

Are we always creating you, as Rilke said,
Trying, on our best days,
To make possible your coming-into-existence?

Or are you merely a story told in the dark,
A child's drawing of barn and star?

Each year you are born again. It is no remedy

For what we go on doing to each other,
For history's blind repetitions of hate and reprisal.

Here I am again, huddled in hope. For what
Do I wait? – I know you only as something missing,
And loved beyond reason.

As a word in my mouth I cannot embody.

II.

On the snow-dusted field this morning – an etching
Of mouse tracks declares the frenzy of its hunger.

The plodding dawn sun rises to another day's
One warm hour. I'm walking to the iced-in local pond

Where my neighbours have sat through the night
Waiting for something to find their jigged lure.

The sky is paste white. Each bush and tree keeps
Its cold counsel. I'm walking head-on into a wind

That forces my breath back into my mouth.
Like rags of black cloth, crows drape a dead oak.

When I pass under them, their cries rip a seam
In the morning. Last week a lifelong friend told me,

There's no such thing as happiness. It's ten years
Since he found his son, then a nineteen year old

Of extraordinary grace and goodness, curled up
In his dormitory room, unable to rise, to free

Himself of a division that made him manic and
Depressed, and still his son struggles from day to day,

The one partial remedy a dismal haze of drugs.
My friend hopes these days for very little – a stretch of

Hours, a string of a few days when nothing in his son's life
Goes terribly wrong. This is the season of sad stories:

The crippling accident, the layoffs at the factory,
The family without a car, without a house, without money

For presents. The sadder the human drama, the greater
Our hope, or so the television news makes it seem

With its soap-opera stories of tragedy followed up
With ones of good will – images of Santa's pots filling up

At the malls, truckloads of presents collected for the shelters,
Or the family posed with their special-needs child

In front of a fully equipped van given by the local dealership.
This is the season to keep the less fortunate in sight,

To believe that generosity will be generously repaid.
We've strung coloured lights on our houses and trees,

And lit candles in the windows to hold back the dark.
For what do we hope? – That our candles will lead you

To our needs? That your gift of light will light
These darkest nights of the year? That our belief

In our own righteousness will be vindicated?
The prophet Amos knew the burden of your coming.

The day of the Lord is darkness, he said, *darkness, not light,*
As if someone went into a house and rested a hand against a wall,

And was bitten by a snake. Amos knew the shame of
What we fail, over and over, to do, the always burning

Image of what might be. Saint Paul, too, saw
The whole of creation groaning for redemption.

And will you *intercede with sighs too deep for words*
Because you love us in our weakness, because

You love always, suddenly and completely, what is
In front of you, whether it is a lake or leper.

Because you come again and again to destroy the God
We keep making in our own image. Will we learn

To pray: May our hearts be broken open. Will we learn
To prepare a space in which you might come forth,

In which, like a bolt of winter solstice light,
You might enter the opening in the stones, lighting

Our dark tumulus from beginning to end?

III.

All last night the tatter of sleet, ice descending,
Each tree sheathed in ice, and then, deeper
Into the night, the shattering cracks and fall
Of branches being pruned by gusts of wind.

It is the first morning after the longest night,
Dawn colourless, the sun still cloud-silvered.
Four crows break the early stillness, an apocalypse
Of raucous squawks. My miniature four horsemen

Take and eat whatever they can in the field
Outside my door: a deer's leg my dog has dragged
Home. Above them, the flinty sun has at last fired
A blue patch of sky, and suddenly each ice-transfigured

Tree shines. Each needle of pine, each branch
Of ash, throws off sparks of light. Once,
A rabbi saw a spark of goodness trapped inside
Each evil, the very source of life for that evil –

A contradiction not to be understood, but suffered,
The rabbi explained, though the one who prays
And studies Torah will be able to release that spark,
And evil, having lost its life-giving source, will cease.

When I finally open my door and walk out
Into the field, every inch of my skin seems touched
By light. So much light cannot be looked at:
My eyelids slam down like a blind.

All morning I drag limbs into a pile. By noon,
The trees and field have lost their shine. I douse
The pile of wood with gas, and set it aflame,
Watching sparks disappear in the sky.

IV.

This is the night we have given for your birth.

After the cherished hymns, the prayers, the story
Of the one who will become peacemaker,
Healer of the sick, the one who feeds
The hungry and raises the dead,

We light small candles and stand in the dark

Of the church, hoping for the peace
A child knows, hoping to forget career, mortgage,
Money, hoping even to turn quietly away

From the blind, reductive selves inside us.

We are a picture a child might draw
As we sing *Silent Night, Holy Night.*

Yet, while each of us tries to inhabit the moment
That is passing, you seem to live in-between
The words we fill with our longing.

The time has come
To admit I believe in the simple astonishment
Of a newborn.

And also to say plainly, as Pascal knew, that you will live
In agony even to the end of the world,

Your will failing to be done on earth
As it is in heaven.

Come, o come Emmanuel,

I am a ghost waiting to be made flesh by love
I am too imperfect to bear.

Paul Murray

O MERCIFUL ONE

When without hope, without aim,
we find ourselves turning and turning
on the outermost rim
of the circumference of our own lives –

When our hearts are cold, our minds
no longer open to the conviction
of the unseen
or to the sources of that conviction –

When words which were fiery
once, electrifying the mind and heart,
now seem but a mimicry of
flame, a dazzle of frozen sparks,

Burn us with your flame of truth,
with your word of love.

Michael Longley

PIETÀ

How compassionate you appear
Bending over your three-year-old
And slipping your little finger
Beneath his penis to lift
The pee-arc away from his clothes.
Did Mary do this for Jesus
Among wood shavings and sawdust?
How tenderly she must have touched.

CAROL

As when the farmer's daughter folds in her jersey
A lamb and bottle, so did the known universe
Come in out of the cold to find her milk warm:
'My lamb,' she crooned to herself. 'My wee lamb.'

Ian Parks

LAZARUS

After I brought you back to life
your short death made you frightened of the sun.
I knelt above you, rolled away the stone,

uncoiled the silken thread that filled your throat.
You never caught my whisper, never saw me when I wept.
I called you from the darkness and you came.

You came expecting birdsong, a new world.
Instead I hauled you up and set you down,
dragged you back choking from the brink.

The others kept their distance, hid their eyes,
refused to hear the flutter of your heart.
You stuttered, disappointed that the world was still the same.

I acted quickly, breathed into your mouth –
astonished as your blue lips turned to red.
I learned your secret, kept it to myself,

stood silent as you stumbled from the cave.
I loved you for returning, for the effort that you'd made.
You hated me for doing what I'd done.

Ruth Padel

from SEVEN WORDS AND AN EARTHQUAKE

THE ULNAR NERVE
The Word of Forgiveness

Olives in blue-tissue mist. Sunrise in the *wadi*
one Friday in spring. Bare creviced hills
pink-threaded with cyclamen and flax,

wild almond in bloom, leaves of the rock
rose, green on grey stone. Three gazelles
on the ridge, running. But you, you're on your back

facing sky like mother-of-pearl in a body
you can't climb out of. If you could turn
your head, you'd see dry

stalks of last winter's grass
lit by rays you feel you could touch.
Rays like ingots of fluff,

spokes of a broken wheel, almost
horizontal, pierce a halo of dust
around visitors coming up

the path from town. Alone
last night at full moon
you prayed so hard your sweat was blood.

Capillaries broke like straw
and leaked into your pores. Handcuffed
you found others to care about. The guard

who whacked you in the mouth
for keeping silent
under questioning. Squaddies

expert in the flay
knotted with lead weights
who sliced skin off your back and shoulders.

Centurions with digital timers posed
by your hooded body. The human genome –
Thumbs-Up-for-Me-with-Chained-Detainee

in-a-Foetal-Position. Anything goes
at the checkpoint, the cell, the interview-room.
Untied, you slumped to paving

purple as Judas
blossom with your blood. A soldier
wove barbed strands of caper bush –

in Hebrew *avionah*, also called Desire,
whose white buds
freckle the slopes at Capernaum

above the Sea of Galilee like talc –
into a crown of claws
and pushed it through the vascular

fretwork of your scalp.
But now you're with the experts. They do this week in
week out – jam someone's naked spine

and scapula, oozing gleams
of opened muscle, against rough-sawn timber
like this lumber you dragged through the city.

They tie your arms to the T-beam
allowing for flexion. *Largo, largo* –
they've been told

to ratchet up the pain.
You can't hope
for the easy option, the hollow

below the wrist, the Only-Use-Metal way
of making sure some nail
won't shred through the hand

and the whole boiling cascade
off the cross. No, with rope
to take your weight

the man with mallet and spike
can penetrate
the star-centre of your palm

where life-curve crosses line of the heart
and the ulnar nerve
begins its delicate run. Each arm

through brachial plexus, root-nerve, nape
and on up the back of your skull
will feel on fire

for the duration, the who-
knows-how-many hours
this Friday business will take.

There's more where that came from,
the whole human brew
of jealousy and spite.

So you displace. You think
of the others. *Father, forgive them*
for they know not what they do.

THE DOUBLE WALL OF THE PERICARDIUM

The Word of Abandonment

What breeds about the smoke-house of the heart?
No more worrying over others. This is it
now, the central ceremony
of let's-not-look-away from the great stone ring
of you on your own, under a rug of flies. Bubble-wrap
of viscid spittle down your chin has dried
like gluey fire consumed by its own ash.
New agony begins: crushing pain in the deep chest.

The fortress membrane, built like the wall
of China as a double palisade to keep in
roots of the *aorta, vena cava*, pulmonary vein
and this *shump shump* of muscle pushing blood

through shattered cells, is silting up with serum
and starts to compress the heart. Where's healing
now? You've lived for others' feelings. You've seen
darkness over earth, the forked stick on the path.

Now it's mucus on the lip, mouths of wounds
peeling to black. Eclipse. You long to melt to air.
This was it, your one shot at experience:
circumference of skin and swirling bitumen
of self. You can't get away from the bedrock
of Shut Out: that feeling there's nobody, not even
to reproach. What you're abandoned by is your own dream.
You believed, whatever else, you were promised.

But this is the ocean floor of all you've been:
that you're alone with pain, that's what you're for.
No angels around now to make wise men go home
by another route, avoiding the jealous king:
the one who persecutes,
the one who says, OK destroy your own.
Untouchable means you're separate.

You trusted to a bond. Mistakenly.
You've no choice but the ancient tongue
called Vulnerability. *Where have you taken me?*
Watch lavender walls of the pericardium
overflow with serum. Shout in a loud voice
and the new metallic-tasting dark translates.
'My God, why have you forsaken me?'

TREE
The Word of Fulfilment

Antlers of sacrifice. A chill creeping through veins
and dying tissue. *Lento, lento*: we can't pretend
it's not happening. There's a smell of burning rubber,
a hiss like static on an ambisonic microphone
and a spine, a bone zip, trying to keep together
what's falling apart. Air like black chiffon
at three in the afternoon

as children are let out of school
to go home. We're all here, in our own
fibonacci sequences of pain, the body in its failures
and mess, sepsis, things that go wrong. But a white
bird comes flashing through karst
of this dark sky like quartz, a needle of light
cutting the human scene in half
to say you're not alone –

everything that separates unites
and yes there was point to all the mire
and godforsakenness. It wasn't just illusion,
hanging in when the going gets tough
shedding a mantle of self.
The rainbow's end is real:
your own slice of *good enough*.
The story, the gash in time begun
with an outcast birth, is never sealed
but you have to feel it all. Fire-bolts of steel
through your palms. There is no *numb*. Tissues tear
in your back when you shift up and down
the emery of rough timber. There's no morphine
to tip in your throat but you're nearly there
and you whisper, *Done. It's done.*

ZIG-ZAGS ON PATTERNS OF SILK FROM SAMARKAND

The Word of Reunion

Who are the guilty? One more breath
enters the lungs. This is neither silence nor speech
but a cross-roads, a sunset at dawn.
Asphyxia. Head on the chest,

the far point of powerlessness
in eyes of a blinded robin. Insects
are siphoning your sap. The to and fro
of arteries and auto-immune-defence

has nearly stopped. What would it be
to join the Other whom you know
is here with you? Will you be swallowed?
Can you give up your soul? Something is slipping free

like the repeated syllable that turned out to be
you learning to talk. Packages of memory
jag and swirl before your eyes: holding her hand
to name the planets, knowing you were small

you were the finite holding the infinite;
or gazing at crimson sky, flame-triangles
of noctilucent cumulus, maroon and white
like zig-zags on patterns of silk from Samarkand

she bought to wrap you in. The crowds below
buzzing like filaments of a clapped-out
electric heater, could be humming lullabies
to fauna of the night: the shy Arabian leopard

and golden spiny mouse of Palestine.
Go where it hurts most. In a last surge
of strength, press your torn feet and severed
metatarsal bone against the nail.

Straighten your knees, inhale
a last deep breath. You're one minute
from home. *Father, into your hands*
I commit my spirit.

Author's Note: The Seven Last Words, or rather Sayings, of Christ on the Cross come from the Gospels. Three from Luke, three from John and one which appears in both Mark and Matthew. They are used in Good Friday sermons and meditations for Holy Week. In 1787, Haydn was commissioned to write an instrumental setting for the sayings, presumably to be performed on Good Friday in Cádiz Cathedral.

Haydn wrote a slow introduction to the seven movements and after the last added an Earthquake movement, probably thinking of the 1755 earthquake which devastated Lisbon and many cities in Portugal and Spain including Cádiz, caused tsunamis from North Africa to Cornwall, and in Ireland partly destroyed the 'Spanish Arch' section of Galway city and flooded the marketplace in Kinsale. It struck on All Saints Day, destroyed nearly all the churches in Lisbon and caused an equally violent aftershock of faith. Voltaire used it in *Candide* and in his 'Poem on the Lisbon disaster' to attack the notion that all is for the best in this world.

Commissioned to write poems between Haydn's movements, I listened to the Haydn again and again, discussed it with musicians, and thought about the emotional arc of the Sayings. The first three, 'Father Forgive them for they know not what they do', 'Verily I say unto you, this night you will be with me in Paradise', and 'Mother, behold thy son; son, behold thy mother', all seemed to me to focus the pain onto others: the torturers, the thief crucified with him, and his mother and friend. Only in the central one, 'My God why has thou forsaken me?', known as the Word of Abandonment, does he start to address his own pain; and only then, it seems, can he admit need. 'I thirst' sums up all need. After admitting his humanity and his need of others, he comes to the Word of Triumph, Fulfilment or Achievement. 'It is done' means (all these interpretations and translations have been endlessly discussed in the literature) he has done what he was put here to do and and now can come home, as it were, to relationship – to Reunion: 'Father into Thy hands I commit my spirit'.

The arc seemed to me to move from displacing unbearable pain onto others, towards admitting it in oneself. Admitting loss, and need of others, empowers him – as maybe it enables everyone – to move on and find a new sense of achievement and reunion.

Haydn's movements are all slow except the earthquake at the end, but subtly differentiated. 'I thirst' for instance has pizzicato strings which suggest the longed-for drops of water. I thought the only way for me to go into this with Haydn as a guide was via the cells, and see what is happening to organs of the body during these hours, so the audience could remember that as they listen to the Haydn. Since the eighteenth century, physicians have speculated about what actually Christ died of, and what was going on in his body as he suffered. I thought I could let that stand for all the other dimensions of feeling.

John O'Donnell

THE STORM

We should have seen it coming, I suppose,
but we were dog-tired when we left, and skies
seemed clear, the sun's work done, sinking astern.
He'd flaked out down below, missing his turn
to steer – and who could blame him, wanting peace
from days of heat and dust, and everywhere
excited hordes, clamouring for a piece
of him. A shame to wake him, but we were
in real trouble, too late to shorten sail,
heaving waves swamping the decks, the boom of gale
enough to raise the dead. I slapped his face:
'We're going down! Don't you care?' He blinked, then stared
as if he'd come back from another place
to wind and water, waiting for his word.

Dragan Dragojlović

FATHER

We opened all the windows on our house,
and we opened the door
waiting for father; a large spider
was spinning its web
around the young morning sun;

the day mellowed by the hour,
the year grew older,
we waited
a whole year round,
then another, and another, and one more,
we waited until we saw
trees in blossom in the garden

as father paced alongside Jesus Christ
watching the flying bees,
while a quaint light
rose toward the sky.

Dragan Dragojlović

MOTHER

She was the best pupil in primary school,
the most beautiful girl before she married
a young man who had many
orchards, meadows and woods,
and countless hectares of land.

She bore three sons,
university graduates,
she and her husband moved house twice,
and built three houses; smartly and patiently
she quelled disputes,
spread kindliness, holding in her heart
a world of love.

With her strength, she could move
the hills,
she toiled away on the estate,
she milked sheep and cows, prepared food,
stopped torrents, dispersed the clouds,
gave wise advice to everyone

and prayed every day, every evening
she knelt at her bedside invoking
God and Jesus Christ.

When her husband died, she still knelt down,
when her first son died, she only prayed,
when her other son died young
she wondered if there was greater despair on earth
when Jesus Christ did not hear her;

now, on a crucifix above her grave,
on holy days,
an unfamiliar bird sings.

Dragan Dragojlović

A DISTANT VOICE

My God, my God, why have you forsaken me?
– Christ at Golgotha

Were that voice
to be heard now,
what would all those years do
that have repeated the same cry
for centuries?
Would it recognise itself
in our prayers?

Were it to be heard now,
what would be the words that could
describe each moment's hope?
How would this day
and this rain behave?

He might be here this very moment,
he might never have departed
from our heart.
Words are heard clearly:
My God,
have mercy on your son
and teach him how to build
a home of love on Earth
where You could come
admitting that you have not forsaken us.

'Father', 'Mother' and 'A Distant Voice' are translated from Serbian by Stanislava Lazarević

Conor McDonough

'OUR GAZE IS SUBMARINE': CLASSICISM AND ROMANTICISM IN ART AND FAITH

'Christian myth is so contentious and exhausted'. So said the late, great, and much-lamented poet, Seamus Heaney in his last published interview. In the case of Ireland, who could deny it? Practice of the Catholic faith here is on the wane, as is belief in key and controversial teachings. Christian moral teaching is selectively accepted – 'yes' to sharing one's toys, 'no' to *Humanae Vitae* – as is teaching on doctrinal matters. In the popular imagination, Irish Catholic topography ranges from the ridiculous (Craggy Island) to the dour (Lough Derg) to the evil (Letterfrack). On the academic scene, theology is a cobwebbed discipline, moth-balled in a few fringe institutions, and certainly not taking its place in the fast-moving mainstream of our 'knowledge economy'.

Most of us will concede, however, that the Church achieves some limited goods. Jesus is usually thought of as a good egg, and, if I may continue my oological theme, the local parish is often thought of as a curate's egg: good in parts. Marking rites of passage, comforting the sick and dying, providing some charitable assistance – these aspects of Christian practice are broadly welcome, even now. But while *goodness* is permitted to attach itself to the Church, that other transcendental, *truth*, is not. The Christian story is received by many of our contemporaries as not only 'contentious and exhausted' but also untrue. Where, then, does this leave people like me, who happen to believe the myth? Should we let the story die? Or should we seek to re-frame the narrative and hear it with fresh ears? If the latter, how should we go about this repristination? So many practices are needful – good catechesis, passionate evangelisation, true community-building – but I think having the right ideas is just as important as engaging in good practices. In trying to discern the basic attitude of mind which serves this renewal, I find it helpful to converse with another poet: Thomas Stearns Eliot.

I first met Eliot's work when I was a student at Cambridge, ten years ago. The 'faith of my fathers' was challenged there at every turn, and I was forced to think and rethink my faith. In this reflection, I found some fine companions: Christopher Dawson, Hans Urs von Balthasar, and above all, G K Chesterton. When I first met Eliot I thought I had found another ally. I had come across Eliot's self-description as a 'classicist in literature, royalist in politics, and Anglo-Catholic in religion' and was intrigued. I wasn't sure what 'classicist' meant in the literary context, I was uninterested in his royalism, but the fact that this great name identified as a 'Catholic' (albeit with a prefix) meant love at first sight: 'flesh of my flesh', another unfashionable Catholic, another ally in my counter-cultural struggles.

Then I turned to his poems. I expected to find rhyming, metrical, sensible texts, something like one of Chesterton's worthy ballads. Surely that was what he meant by 'classicist in literature'. What I found, of course, was something entirely different: shifting perspectives, opaque meaning ('Swelling to maculate giraffe'?), repetitions, quotations, unpredictable metre. Yet for all their strangeness, I read and re-read the poems, and they continued to intrigue me. How could such unorthodox forms count as 'classicism'? Where was the voice of the poet among all these quotations? I was haunted by questions, but haunted even more by Eliot's words: 'The worlds revolve like ancient women / Gathering fuel in ancient lots'; 'I should be glad of another death'; 'What seas what shores what granite islands towards my timbers / And woodthrush calling through the fog / My daughter'.

When broaching mysteries of the faith, too, Eliot chose unusual words: Christ on the cross is a 'wounded surgeon', Bethlehem is 'satisfactory'. Even the Litany of Our Lady is rendered unsettling: 'Lady of silences / Calm and distressed / Torn and most whole / Rose of memory / Rose of forgetfulness / Exhausted and life-giving / Worried reposeful'. My putative ally had fixed me with an unexpected look, and I didn't know what to say.

If his work doesn't constitute a cosy ghetto of familiar messages and images, what, then, does Eliot have to offer his Christian reader? For my part, I found it helpful to turn to his prose, to discover how *he* understood his poetry, and the nature of poetry itself. Above all in 'Tradition and the Individual Talent', I found an arresting vision of literary work, with a key binary at its heart. Considered under its different aspects, this binary can be formulated as 'tradition' vs. 'novelty', 'impersonality' vs. 'personality', or 'imitation' vs. 'invention'. Eliot consciously and consistently set himself against the Romantic tendency to privilege the second half of this binary. On the Romantic account of art, the artist strives *not* to imitate, but to produce original work by sheer dint of 'genius'. This genius is simply a gift, and to be sharply contrasted from mere erudition, as in the formulations of the early Romantic, Edward Young: 'Learning we thank, genius we revere'; 'Genius is from Heaven, learning from man'; 'Learning is borrowed knowledge; genius is knowledge innate, and quite our own'.

In contrast with the Romantic vision, Eliot refuses to praise novelty and individuality in poets. For him, poetic art involves not self-assertion but self-negation: 'The progress of an artist is a continual self-sacrifice, a continual extinction of personality.' Cheap imitation, especially imitation of the previous generation, is, of course, to be rejected. Eliot proposes something more thoroughgoing; entering into the poetic tradition involves 'great labour': a poet should 'write not merely with his own generation in his bones, but with a feeling that the whole of the literature of Europe from Homer and within it the whole of the literature of his own country has a simultaneous existence and composes a simultaneous order'. Failing to attempt this labour sets the poet on the wrong track, seeking perhaps 'for new human emotions to express'. But the poet who *has* achieved this initiation into tradition must then be understood in that light: 'No poet [...] has his complete meaning alone. His significance, his appreciation is the appreciation of his relation to the dead poets and artists. You cannot value him alone; you must set him, for contrast and comparison, among the dead.'

Reading these words, I realised that Romantic assumptions about art were deeply implanted in my own consciousness. I had thought of artistic imitation as craven, and artistic anonymity seemed to me a contradiction in terms. Writers of pseudepigrapha weren't *real* writers, the anonymous composers of Gregorian chant weren't *real* musicians, and artists in rigid traditions (like iconographers in the Eastern Christian world, or miniaturists in the Persian and Ottoman empires) weren't *real* artists. After reading Eliot, though, I began to question my Romantic assumptions. I began to reinterpret these dead works as living expressions of a tradition, carrying a greater significance than that transmitted by mere authorial intention. I began to sample the ancient, medieval, and early modern literature which formed the tradition of which Eliot spoke, and my horizons were broadened. I had been converted from Romanticism to Classicism: I began to read books now not as individual creations, but as members of a community of texts. With Eliot as my guide, I had made the journey, you might say, from the book to the library.

Nevertheless, one hundred years after Eliot wrote 'Tradition and the Individual Talent', the Romantic attitude is surely even more entrenched, in art and life, than it was in his time. The self-maker and the mould-breaker are treasured types in our imaginary. 'Change' is so unequivocally positive in connotation that it can function as a political slogan without qualification. Reading Eliot has made me aware of, and suspicious of, these assumptions, above all in an ecclesial context, for everywhere Romantic attitudes to faith abound. This is surely the basic position of one who self-designates as 'spiritual but not religious' or who says 'I like Jesus but not the institutional church'. The very separation between the 'institutional church' and some putative spirit of primitive Christianity can be understood as an essentially Romantic attitude. It seems to me, though, that Romantic Catholicism is a self-subverting enterprise: Catholicism always involves a commitment to repetition – the same proclamation of faith, the same prayers, the same gestures – for the word 'catholic' means 'universal', and this catholicity runs through time as well as space. But such repetition represents to the Romantic attitude mere spiritual slavery. If the Catholic tree is to bear fruit again, it will need to find better soil than rocky Romanticism.

Step forward Classicism which, like Romanticism, can be an attitude to life as much as to art. If Romanticism takes the individual as its starting point, Classicism begins with the community. It is called 'traditionalism' or 'conservatism', often with pejorative overtones. Under its negative aspect it is narrow-minded, fogeyish, unadventurous, but Chesterton summarised the positive aspect of this attitude when he spoke of tradition as 'the democracy of the dead'. Just as the classicist poet should have 'the whole of the literature of Europe' in his bones, so the traditionalist seeks wisdom, not first of all in her own bright ideas, but in the great works of reflection. She should, in Chesterton's words again, seek to think through 'thought that has been thought out'.

How would such an attitude play out with respect to Catholicism? Most obviously, it would rule out the Romantic attitude outlined above. If we situate ourselves firmly within the tradition of the Church then 'being spiritual' (relating to God) necessarily involves 'being religious' (acting, praying, thinking in concert with the whole Church). The classical attitude includes also the willingness to engage rigorously with the texts and practices which we have received – Scripture, the Fathers, Councils, the schoolmen, the lives of the saints, the liturgy, devotions – and to see these not as disconnected artefacts, but as composing a 'simultaneous order'. It involves, above all, suppressing the desire to select favourite elements of the faith. Instead, the classical Christian must say 'Yes' to Old Testament *and* New Testament, to Gospels *and* Epistles, to St Thomas Aquinas *and* St Thérèse, to Vatican I *and* Vatican II. If the classical poet engages in 'a continual extinction of personality', so too the classical Christian submits his own insights to the insights of the tradition.

If, dear reader, your veins are about to burst at this horrible prospect, tell your Inner Romantic to calm down. My own I.R. points out the obvious danger in the classical attitude to Christianity: it can involve making an idol of cultural artefacts, and neglecting the immediate experience of God. My Inner Classicist calmly responds: 'We humans live, learn, talk and think in community; in the next life we will see God face to face, but now we are wayfarers, and we come at Him *through* the icons – not idols – of the tradition which he inaugurated, and which he guides.'

Eliot shows the classical attitude at work in his 'Choruses from "The Rock"' better than I can in fumbling prose:

O Light Invisible, we praise Thee!
Too bright for mortal vision.
O Greater Light, we praise Thee for the less;
The eastern light our spires touch at morning,
The light that slants upon our western doors at evening,
The twilight over stagnant pools at batflight,
Moon light and star light, owl and moth light,
Glow-worm glowlight on a grassblade.
O Light Invisible, we worship Thee!

We thank Thee for the lights that we have kindled,
The light of altar and sanctuary;
Small lights of those who meditate at midnight
And lights directed through the coloured panes of windows
The gilded carven wood, the coloured fresco.
Our gaze is submarine, our eyes look upward
And see the light that fractures through unquiet water.
We see the light but see not whence it comes.
O Light Invisible, we glorify Thee!

'Our gaze is submarine'. The Greater Light gives us sight, but in this life we see it only refracted and coloured by water and glass, reflected by wood and paint, transmitted by translucent generations of believers. The myriad of lesser lights which results constitutes the Christian tradition we receive. The classical attitude, as I have proposed it, makes astronomers of Christians: our 'great labour' is to discern constellations in these lights, to discover the 'simultaneous order' which bespeaks the unity of the Greater Light from which the lesser lights derive, and towards which we stargazers journey. If old texts, old words and old gestures deserve to be polished up to serve the renewal of Christianity in Ireland, it is because they remain privileged conduits from the ever-new Source which gives to poet and disciple alike an ever-new tongue.

Paul Perry

JESUS AS A YOUNG HUNGARIAN DEAF WOMAN CIRCA 1940

The windows were tiny and the train started.
At night the train stopped.
We got off.

We lay down in a huge yard.
We received this uniform, put a kerchief on our heads;
everybody retained their shoes.

It was odd to be bald.
Everybody was very cold.
I got scared because I found some lice.

It was strange.
The other women's legs were swollen.
We were working in the mud,

Sweeping the area in January.
There were officers sitting at a table –
My sister warned me.

Somebody said, 'Don't you like the deaf?'
I said, 'I listen to my sister.'
I was sent out to dig the graves.

I was the 'crier'.
My hands were hurting ...
It was cold.

I wasn't strong.
My sister was much stronger than me.
I was digging the graves.

We were fighting.
We stole from each other.
The last grave I dug was my own.

Ned Balbo

DEAD MAN WALKING

John 11:1-12:50

At first he was a sideshow: the dead man raised,
someone to gawk at during his three squares
or trips back from the privy: *he's alive,*
all right – reason to think about those rumours
and strange sayings making all the rounds
before you draw conclusions that they're bunk.
But, later, it was strange: back from the dead,
whatever chamber held him, he seemed lost –
as if the Man from Nazareth and he
had shared some secret no one should endure,
and he was left behind to bear the mark.
My job was keeper, plainclothes guardian,
and model convert: stationed at his home,
I'd lead the tour groups over for a look
at him, Christ's greatest miracle so far,
then lead them out, careful to watch for signs
that marked them allies – traitors, possibly –
though most were only curious: fellow Jews
still on the fence, willing to be convinced.
He'd tear the bread, dip it in olive oil,
and chew – he'd chew so thoroughly, I'd want
to shake him by the sleeve, 'Enough already!'
crumbs stuck in his beard, but turned away
instead to talk with those who watched, inspired.
The sisters, Martha and Mary, ran the house –
they, their servants, and some hangers-on –
what good could *he* do, wandering at will,
vanished for hours, sometimes on the day
he knew I'd show him off; I'd stall for time
with shepherds, moneylenders grown impatient
for the proof that we'd exchange for faith.
(I lost more than a few of them that way.)
Why him? What were we getting for the deal?
The rest of us, I felt, deserved some scrap
of what his afterlife, or lack of it,
had shown: the secrets he was holding back.

I thought of my dead wife, my only daughter,
a few more who'd have better suited me
to make the trip, if I'd had any say ...
I didn't, and they haven't to this day.
Another week, another round of doubters,
lousy conversation, worst of all
the resurrected host's, and my small place
in Someone's great plan hidden from us all.
And then, the sideshow wrapped; the curtain closed.
Some said: Apostles' orders, others told
me that the Pharisees had placed a contract
on his head since he inspired belief,
having, you know, once come back from the dead.
Good luck the second time, I thought to say,
but checked myself: what was the latest Word,
brought back with loaves and palm-branch souvenirs?
He that hates his life here in this world
will live eternally. Did that explain
why Lazarus had grown so loathe to speak,
unnerving even those who loved him once –
Mary, who washed his feet and rubbed his joints,
Martha, who brewed the heavy lentil soup
in which he dipped his bread – and me, of course,
though love was not the feeling that I harboured.
Sometimes I think about the time I found him
standing off the road to Bethany,
some weed-choked precipice where I rushed forward,
grabbed his wrist and pulled him back to earth
to face our wrath, his duty, and the long
walk back. He answered 'Nothing' every time
I asked what he'd been doing, what he saw.
Maybe it's good he kept us in the dark.
As lookout, go-fer, keeper of the Faith's
corporeal proof, now stuck with other tasks
essential to the Cause, I'm guaranteed,
whatever rage the dead man made me feel,
I'll know – as he will, too – eternal life.

William Wenthe

A LESSER STORY

My trouble with the historical dead
is the way they always come to us
complete, fledged with full resumé
of deeds, each one a tableau of self
accomplished: with palette or sword;
wearing the iconic headdress – tricorn,
black beret, coonskin cap, or crown

of thorns. Yes, you. More than anyone,
you've been given to me since childhood
as alpha and omega of fulfillment:
magical babe printed on cards, perfected
sufferer nailed above an altar,
never far from the beam of light
that overwrites all wounds with
the happy ending of *The Greatest Story* ...

And your nonchalance of loaves and fishes,
your hem-of-the-garment lauds
for others' modesty – even in humility
you are pedestalled; and how we reverence
your wrath that rectified the temple.
I gave that one a try, not long ago:
called out the hypocrites, manipulators –
the moneychangers, so to speak,
in my place of work. What a supreme
failure that was – they only fattened
on my fury, and I became the fool.

But now that I am washed in
the abrasive eyewash of humiliation,
I think I can see you, thoroughly
stripped of your story. As for being
endorsed as the son of God, I wouldn't know;
but haven't we both understood
how it is to be spurned by *persons*,
to be called *poser*? Surely I've never been
scourged as you were, but I believe

you might have felt, beneath the blood
inflicted by whips, the seep of your own,
self-generated, sweat of unworthiness.

And would you know then, too, the feeling,
the tempest within, of not knowing
who you are? Lord – Stranger –
stop with me here. Let's grab an empty table
and meet: you, me, some wine,
and the unstoried pain
of becoming man.

Paddy Bushe

TO JESUS ON THE CROSS

In the name of all
                    that's holy on the earth
let yourself be taken down.
                              There has not been
nor will there be
                    an answer to that third hour
howl of forsakenness
                         to a darkening sky
that no divine claptrap
                         will ever lighten.
Let yourself be taken down
                              and let us hear
what you
          and the weeping women
                                   and the soldiers
have to say, humanly
                    and
                         humanly, let us pray.

Philip McDonagh

THE MOCKERY

The lads knew all the risks. It helped our singing
together, on the run. The awful thing
was what it did to women. A full show,
the scourge, the nails, the end coming so slow
– for wife or child even to hear of it
was ruin. We in the movement did our bit
for condemned men, but stationing someone there?
The lads nailed up were usually past caring.
This pig of a hot day, I noticed one
woman who stood within just yards of her son
hoisted with our lads over jerking spears.
She told us later our dead volunteers'
questions, their struggled-for words, had been an act
of friendship; and her son would not retract
friendship, though one poor lad may have lost his head.
The real sin was the Roman show, she said.
Dogs' work. A mockery. A thing obscene.
So yes, I do remember the Galilean.

Philip McDonagh

DE-CONSTRUCTING SILENCE

Silence they had construed as our consent:
the Romans never looked for some quintessence
of loyalty. Wrong though it may have been,
I took to that dull stage of the Sanhedrin,
performed a secondary part well, clung
to my effectiveness, and ruled my tongue.
No one could know the fears we left unsaid,
the harbours of grief that stayed unvisited.
With heavy calculations we had laden
our word-carrying ships. We had no trade
in the untreated fact. Why choose to inflame
old injury, by giving truth its name?
The day good Nicodemus asked me come
join him and plead at the praetorium,
a noise that had been buzzing in my ears
through all the meetings and down all the years
turned into music. Something we made start
within the Roman governor's tomb-like heart.

Philip McDonagh

RENUNCIATION

For such a big beginning, the hour seemed right:
the first day of the week, the end of night.
Today, the story has been written down,
this way or that; and though he said, 'tell no one,'
of certain things, I will spill out this much,
it knocked me back, the way he said 'don't touch';
just like that other time in Capernaum,
he wasn't yet on the road, and yes, I saw him
as someone I could be with. 'If my right eye,'
he said, 'bathed in some brightness too nearby,
makes me shoot wide, forget even my aim,
better the eyes of ragged men and lame
who hit on the true mark.' I had tried to probe
towards who he was, put on him a royal robe,
for better or worse. That morning in the garden,
the truth came home to me. I felt his pardon
as I held back, and then the recompense
of mixing our two lives, in a new sense.

Philip McDonagh

HORN AND IVORY

> One is made of ivory, the other made of horn [...]
> The dreams that pass through the gates of polished horn
> Are fraught with truth ...
> – *Odyssey*, 19.634-638

We were beginning to wonder, I won't deny it,
if in the end the authorities were right:
a destitute presenting as a king
was too outlandish, a dream entering
through the gate of ivory, we Greeks would say;
and so we left the city on that same day.
The stranger on the road with whom we shared
all this – how we'd backed off and hadn't dared
attend those meetings or commit to him
– turned round to indicate Jerusalem
as the sun set and quoted text on text
until we lost ourselves. Though not perplexed,
we had no words. The sorrow of the Messiah,
his gentleness, and how in Zechariah
he rides in wobbling on a donkey, seemed
obvious as a thing you knew you'd dreamed
and in the dreaming knew – as what we read
afterwards, in the breaking of the bread.

Philip McDonagh

THE CHOICE OF MEDIUM

The slave is answerable in his body:
more than a maxim when you've seen the rod-
and scourge-marks, the lifelong disfigurement
of man, woman, and child. With backs half-bent,
they kept old slave-stripes out of our eyes' way
in that assembly in Trastevere;
yet when I spoke of the devil as a ring
of lock-stepping souls, not crediting
the moves of mercy; as bloated prestige,
bustable power; and said his name was 'Legion',
our slaves made in the legionary wars
out East could only laugh. This was applause,
so the other thing I asked our people to note
is how the Master, knowing the psalms by rote,
and every theory and every storyline,
chose for his medium the bread and wine:
Abraham's God, Isaac's and Joseph's God,
was answerable in this body and blood.

Seamus Heaney

THE LATECOMERS

He saw them come, then halt behind the crowd
That wailed and plucked and ringed him, and was glad
They kept their distance. Hedged on every side,

Harried and responsive to their need,
Each hand that stretched, each brief hysteric squeal –
However he assisted and paid heed,

A sudden blank letdown was what he'd feel
Unmanning him when he met the pain of loss
In the eyes of those his reach had failed to bless.

And so he was relieved the newcomers
Had now discovered they'd arrived too late
And gone away. Until he hears them, climbers

On the roof, a sound of tiles being shifted,
The treble scrape of terra cotta lifted
And a paralytic on his pallet

Lowered like a corpse into a grave.
Exhaustion and the imperatives of love
Vied in him. To judge, instruct, reprove,

And ease them body and soul.
Not to abandon but to lay on hands.
Make time. Make whole. Forgive.

Eiléan Ní Chuilleanáin

TEACHING DAILY IN THE TEMPLE

The crowd in its bunches, men near me,
Some women hunkered low on the ground,
A child at the breast, one girl standing tense
As an archer focusing – why should I recall them all
(And even a thin man distracted looking away)
And still I can't recover the moment just
When he took and opened the book and began
Reading?
                    or so I gathered

By the way their attention changed.
I heard, *If you knew what the words meant*
In the prophecy of Hosea. Then the noise
Of readying the sacrifice began. I was there,
And so was the column of the Court of Women
Solid between him and me. The offerings flowed
Into the treasury beside the chair, where
He opened the book.

If you knew what this means.
They were angry then and picked up stones to throw,
And he hid away from them, so that day he escaped.
In my memory there is an interlocking
Clutch of enclosures fitted together: the burnt
Offerings, the altar of incense, the loaves
Of proposition on the table for the priests,
Gates and thresholds as pure

As water washes.
The wall of the inner court was tall and blank:
A clean place, nothing growing, the water
From the spring and the cisterns running off
With the blood of sacrifice. The coloured veil
Ruffled in the breeze. And in among them,
Between those barriers, the book now closed

And the phrase I missed
Still there in the coded
Labyrinth I must infiltrate again,
The language of the scroll construe, hunt down
Between those hedges an escaping prey
Before night falls on the phrase, on the lips
That move in the grave.

Mark Jarman

THE TEACHABLE MOMENT

John 18:38

Pilate questioned Jesus.
Jesus questioned back.
Pilate questioned him again –
The cool Socratic tack.

Their repartee was candid,
A pointed give-and-take.
It was not clear if its last word
Was freely willed or fated.

When Jesus chose to answer
And give the reason why,
Pilate asked him, 'What is truth?'

*

Enough about the distant posting among barbarians,
Enough about having to arbitrate their quarrels,
Enough about their religions – about any religion –
Enough about whatever was going on at home, with the family,
When it came time for the intellectual push and pull
He had everything covered, riposte and response,
The tools of dialectic, a question for a question.
He said no more to this princeling of an obscure cause
But turned to the crowd and asked them what they wanted.
Did he win the debate? Do as fated? Make a cosmic mistake?

*

Inside me I believe there is
A Pilate questioning Jesus
And a Jesus answering.
Or no Pilate. Or no Jesus.

*

These two people, powers of their time,
Faced off like a major city and an earthquake.
The city has endured so many earthquakes,
The earthquake's always virgin with a city.
One says it's coming, one must rather doubt it.
And the city shakes down on its tens of thousands.
But here's the thing, the city is rebuilt
With the same name, perhaps with earthquake codes.
The earthquake will not come again for centuries.
And the city stands again, where it has stood.
No wonder the city doubts its own destruction.
How can you live, except to doubt your death?

*

To feel your whole body is the truth,
To feel you are the truth and more than truth,
Your feet, your toes, the shinbone and the knee
Are true and more than true, to be the truth,
Standing on your own feet, and riding hips
As true as they were ever meant to be,
The rest going upward, through the groin,
The functional, true genitals, the belly
Spread with its pubic hair all true, all true,
And up the ridged divided abdomen,
Between the nipples, truly loving touch,
The clavicles with their delicacy and music,
The arms and hands and fingers with their reach,
The tower of the neck, as Solomon says,
The identifiable face, *your* face,
The ears to hear both the outer and inner voices,
The mouth, the speaker of the truth, the nose,
True to its compass bearings, smelling falsehoods,
The eyes looking into the puzzled eyes
Of one you've scared into urgent reasoning –
To feel that you embody the whole truth
And then to know that truth is going to be beaten,
Beaten to the bone, skeletonised,
And hang like a limp rag, as dead as rope –
To be this truth completely, unadorned,
Real as the hand before another's face,
And have that other still say, 'What is truth?'

*

But there is more.
There's always more.
The score's not settled.
There is more.

One shuts the door.
One strikes the door,
Worried, nettled,
Outside the door.

What is truth for?
What is it for
For those who worry
What it is for?

Who pace the floor,
The shifting floor
Of air and fury,
Like a classroom floor.

Who mark the hour,
The frozen hour
Of the last word,
As the first hour?

And what is power
That once was power
In an old word
With a new power?

*

The teachable moment.
The last judgment occurring
Again and again as a teachable moment.
But what moment ever lasted long enough
To learn anything? This moment.

Rowan Williams

STATIONS OF THE GOSPEL

I

All music twisted in one string:
reach out with your long nail,
touch. Listen.

II

Poured from this stone, the water
stings, the mind lurches, suspects
joy, chaos.

III

The wind passes
no sentence: carries scent, sound,
a face felt in the dark.

IV

Thirst drops in the long
dark, swallowed cold by the eager
earth-streaked water.

V

In the deep pool
what fish is wandering through, to make
the dead limbs ripple?

VI

Bread's flavours: sand,
grass, salt, stone, blood, an open cut
from the shore's litter.

VII

Hands close on absence,
broken waters from the cave
beneath the ribs' vault.

VIII

Before all journeys
there is the desert sky, glass-
clear, ice-resonant.

IX

Light catches the slicked
sand, ash, glances behind shut
eyes, opens a wound.

X

No no. Dusting away dazed
flies, he forces the lock;
snow blows in.

XI

Acid tears fall, corrode rocks
in foam, burn away
in shock the grave's knots.

XII

The bowl glows in the furnace.
Inside, beads of sweat
spit and scatter.

XIII

On the worn shiny
boards the water runs, salt with
refuse from dark roads.

XIV

Door swings in the wind:
empty path, low sun ahead
blinds, slows steps, welcomes.

XV

Knifelike, the spring gales
peel skin from sour flesh shrinking
from the candid sun.

XVI

Long secret ends: blood-
smeared, a crown breaks the heaving
of the body's sea.

XVII

Stand here
before the mirror where you see
only the sun behind you.

XVIII

Splinters on paving
stone, red smears; through the window
foreign words stumbling.

XIX

Behind the soldiers' backs
the cloth tears slowly, soaked, eaten
with sour wine.

XX

Put your ears to the crusted gash
in stone or flesh; the mouth
speaks your name.

XXI

Catch it, catch it. The lake
brims over in the bright dawn,
runs from my hands.

Author's Note: This sequence of verses, loosely in haiku form, though with some variations, follows through the twenty-one chapters of St John's Gospel, looking for a focal metaphorical moment in each chapter that gathers the multiple meanings of what the chapter says.

David Harsent

TRICKSTER CHRIST

His image on the water, then the man; they laughed to see it,
but soon fell silent. The storm died round him. The boat
settled into the calm, those aboard wide-eyed. And what
do you think I am, he asked, if not decoy, if not storm-light,
if not lure, if not dream-stock, if not black to your white?

★

Spittle and clay on the eyes of the cureless blind.
They laughed as the world returned.
They stared at each other's faces, wild and dumb.
The sudden blaze of daylight all but blinded them.

★

The stench of the grave still on him. A voice
called him by name as if he were first and last.
He came out in his shroud, laughing behind the gauze.
A seethe of worms ran on his flesh and fell
from his fingertips. A table was set for the feast.
The dead man sat down with the rest and ate his fill.

★

She stooped to touch and a jolt ran through him. She stooped
and caught the hem, finger and thumb. She stooped and left
the print of herself. An issue of blood twelve years: it stopped.
In that self-same moment he turned to her and laughed.

★

At the Pool of Bethesda, in broad daylight, a man
laughing a laugh meant for himself alone
as he walked away: half-lost in the crowd, then gone.

★

That roarer who cut himself with stones for love of pain,
who bedded down on tombs, who broke his chains
and howled and went naked, whose laughter was all delight
for the way he was, who felt the fight
go out of him with the mad stampede downhill
as if he should be speechless and shamed and meek and well.

*

The Mary of seven devils: he turned them out
from each of the seven portals; she bled and laughed and wept.
Later she walked at his side, no longer the slut
though his hand on the dip of her back was surely the start
of whatever would come to her that night as she slept.

Sinéad Morrissey

THE SECOND COMING OF CHRIST

I.

The summer my mother joined the Seventh-day Adventists –
announcing over dinner that Saturday was the Sabbath
and the practice of Sunday worship, an invention of Rome –

the stock-markets crashed in August. I'd been off work
for weeks, keeping immaculate house, craning my neck to catch
the sea's inhalation at the rim of the village,

its ochre-bouldered aftermath, and thinking too much
of the black-edged photograph in Orlando Figes's *A People's Tragedy*
of women of the 'former classes' in the winter of 1919,

selling whatever they owned on the streets of St Petersburg.
Carpets, samovars, oyster knives, if they existed,
have long since been bartered for bread. Instead, they proffer

a coat or a blanket, three spoons, a dinner plate,
at the rag-end of what can be done without,
though one of them still wears a veil, as though to block the shame

of people passing, or of who she used to be, or both.
Riots broke out across London. My children quarrelled and cried.
It rained. I cooked pancakes for breakfast and omelettes

for lunch and our daughter started to speak in sentences:
me me go upstairs now no. Our first-born stopped waking up
in the night after dreams of volcanoes and birds.

II.

I looked up Seventh-day Adventism on the Internet:
a sect that expects the second coming of Christ
and which enjoys the greatest life-expectancy of any sub-group

in America. There are questions I still haven't asked –
if she no longer accepts Darwin, for instance,
or if the Word of God came down to her in a dream

or brought her to her knees with trembling.
I can't imagine it: Jesus back amongst us, recognisably
Himself, but presumably she's expecting it –

cities razed, fields piled high with bodies, the seas on fire
and then a great light streaming from the sky
as when He ascended, visible to everyone in a single instant,

while trumpets sound. Or if, with other Millenarians,
she thinks the saved will be whisked off
like wheat from chaff or froth from milk or hailstones in reverse

in the shutting of the aperture between one second and the next.
I stack the dishwasher twice a day, give my children baths,
sweep the floor in the kitchen when they've gone to sleep

and consider the steady eradication of what's bearable –
ransacked flats, furniture axed for firewood – the likelier scenario.
Come the Rapture, not me, nor any of my kind, will be taken up.

Armand Garnet Ruffo

INDIAN JESUS CHRIST, 1974

Once again he is the blessed child
in the midst of adoration, exaltation:
Our Father Who Art In Heaven.
As his knees grind into the wood floor
and a throbbing ache moves up his legs
and drips off his upper lip,
into his cupped hands.

Staring up to the stained-glass Christ
above the priest and altar
he tries to focus on the one ray of light
filtering through halo and flame
like the divine spirit Himself
so that he might rise up to the rafters
and beyond into cool heaven.

The prayer for salvation never comes to pass.
Christ and his legion of angels
never once lift the roof off the chapel,
carry him up in a chorus of hallelujahs.
Morrisseau is left to find his own wings
and he does, painting his own remembering,
his hands bursting into holy acrylic pain.

– from *The Thunderbird Poems: The Art of Norval Morrisseau*
(Insomniac Press, 2014)

Author's Note: While Norval Morrisseau's grandfather was an Ojibway Shaman, his grandmother was a devout Catholic, and the artist himself attended a Catholic residential school. He spoke of brainwashing and confusion when asked about Christianity. Critics have pointed to the direct influence of stained glass and religious iconography on his painting technique.

Andrew Hudgins

ONE EASTER

After the extended winter,
but buffered still in fleece
against the blunt wind's blasting
in sunlight strangely from the east
as if riding its own cold laughter,
I encountered walking toward me
a worker, gaunt, his hands
bandaged. Sawdust and shavings
topped his hair and eyebrows
like old snow on a lintel,
and as we neared I saw
brown blood dotted
his Carhartts and scarred boots.
As one does, I nodded.
Recognition – call it love –
lit his fixed eyes, then mine –
and I said without knowing
I spoke until I heard it:
You carried the cross for me?
Yes, he, without hesitating,
said, and we passed each
into the other, I
entering a bright tunnel
and he a dark one, beyond
the steady pacing of minutes
and millennia. Through
his clean, clear torment
I, haunted, went hunting
and found only peace, pain,
bloodied love, and a lead
figurine of me nailed
to a living wall. Under
my palm, my nailed self
throbbed. The saviour's heart
beat was my heartbeat,
one indivisible blood-pulse,
weak, then strong and stronger,
until, suddenly cold, I was out

on the Easter street again,
outside the shelter of his suffering
and its warmth, our beating heart
weak now even in memory,
even my own unpredictable
heartbeat lost to me at times –
for seconds, days or decades
released into a retreating
world and laughing wind.

Penelope Shuttle

HOUR'S GHOST

You can learn a lot sitting at a café table
as the hours go by
like a sports channel with the sound turned down,
or by walking about the dull and dreary streets,
past a hand-care carwash,
a candle warehouse,
pondering a choice of four breakfasts
on a bright and bouncy summer morning,
Wandsworth *en fleur*,
wild red roses along a canal bank,
knowing your hours are ghost hours,
you knew that already,
hour's ghost at a door
wreathed in hemlock, nightshade,
hinges and nails red with rust.
Jesus and the Virgin Mary
are dancing on the edge of the world.
It breaks your beating stone heart
as you walk at random
past a row of old almshouses,
a woolshop parachuted-in from the Fifties,
or sit in a café in Battersea,
listening to the voices halt and lame,
the hours going by.

Penelope Shuttle

HOURGLASSES IN THE CHURCH AT JUKKASJÄRVI

There are four of us.
May we never be parted.

You have to stretch up tall
to get a good look at us,

or climb a flight
of pious worn wooden steps,

keeping a sharp eye
on Mary of Lapland,

all golden plaits
and peasant skirts,

dancing with sunburst baby Jesus,
poppy of joy for a sacred heart.

Fixed in our birchwood frame,
we have good work to do,

measuring words,
sermons and sighs,

almost-silence of snowfall,
north wind bragging from his armchair of ice,

hosannas of the river in thaw,
days that are one long noon-brightness,
pitch-dark nights not even a full moon can leaven –

we measure all these.

Tilt us headlong,
shift the quick sands through us –
see, we are making everything *the past*,

the present moment
the mote
neither you nor I nor my three sisters

can single out and say –
this is *now*.

Author's Note: In March 2008 I went on a short trip to Sweden with an old friend. We spent two bright cold days in Stockholm, enjoying a boat ride around the harbour, wrapped in blankets, sitting on reindeer skins, drinking *glühwein* and sampling the famous pea soup. We wandered around the old town, saw the building where the Nobel Prizes are awarded, and went to the beautiful gilded Art Nouveau Opera House where we saw two one-act operas, *The Nightingale* by Stravinsky, and *L'heure espagnole* by Ravel. But delightful as this part of the visit was, the main purpose of our trip was to spend two further days in the far north of Sweden, up in Swedish Lapland.

On our third day we flew up to Kiruna (200 km north of the Arctic Circle), and arrived by mini-van at The Ice Hotel at Jukkasjärvi in the same bright sunshine. To explore the area we were issued with snow-suits to withstand the below-zero temperatures. Walking across the wide and frozen-solid Torne River was an extraordinary experience, as was our snow-shoe walk on Mount Puimonen, and the midnight snow-mobile trip along the Torne and into the forest where we saw the Northern Lights and also had elk stew for supper in a cabin in the woods.

But among all these experiences, and of that of the Ice Hotel itself (which thaws every spring and is rebuilt each autumn from ice harvested during the winter and held in a huge refrigerated warehouse in preparation), it was our visit to the little church of Jukkasjärvi which is most vivid in my recall. This, we discovered, was the oldest church in Lapland. The Sámi people are the indigenous people of Lapland, and they were converted late to Christianity. The church is made of wood, the exterior painted a bright red. Inside we found a number of vigorous and colourful folk-art-style paintings portraying the Christian story from a Sámi perspective. I was struck, particularly, by the big wooden pulpit painted in sky blue and soft rose, ornamented with lines of gilding. Several steps led up to the canopied pulpit. Fastened to one side of the pulpit was a beautiful set of four hourglasses. I'd never seen this in any other church. I liked the assurance and the wit of the installed hourglasses, for surely they were a warning to any preacher not to try the patience of the congregation too far!

The church had a beautiful quiet vitality about it, and it has stayed with me and does stay with me longer than many other recollections of our trip. I've tried, in my poem, to capture the atmosphere of that tiny church so far in the north, and so bright and colourful in its witness and history.

Patricia McCarthy

BRIDES OF CHRIST

We step-danced along: miniature brides of Christ
in white, all betrothed – underage – to the same man.
Críst limm, Críst reum, Críst im degaid.

The Corpus Christi procession on the wet street
spun into a wedding cake's silver ribbon as we became
fantasy queens in the mirrors of our patent pumps.

So many incarnations He had at the intersection
of timelessness with Time: in our own fathers
at night prayers; in green-backed catechisms

whose words pattered by rote concocted him
as suffering little children to come unto him,
yet de-created him if an answer was wrong.

Críst indium, Críst issum, Críst úassum
To the old Irish we clung when a bishop in purple
slapped our cheeks. The heart of our betrothed

hung, sacred, like a donor organ, bleeding from walls
of grottoes. In silent school retreats we grew
closer to him when the priest spelt out each second

of his Passion, each station of his cross. Our own hearts
bled while we swapped holy pictures in his likeness
to slip into missals, or stick on the insides of desk lids

along with pop idols, then prayed for stigmata
like his. *Kyrie Eleison, Christe Eleison*, we chanted.
Críst i illus, Críst i ssius, Críst i n-érus …

debutante polyglots without choice, long dresses
spotless from confessions which wiped slates clean,
sins invented for penances to do on our knees.

Down decades devoid of incense and flowers,
we trampled our net veils into the arid ground of doubt,
tore up apologetics that countered logic, estranged

from him who had taken back his gift – of Faith.
Our handbags, snakeskin-covered now,
hold our turnings away from the *Via Dolorosa*.

Yet in our minds' secret naves, we never forget
Críst i ngiun cach oín rodom labrathar as we take
halting steps of the jig back along the Original Way.

Author's Note: Words in Old Irish are quotations from
'Saint Patrick's Breastplate'.

Michael Augustin

ZU DRITT

Komisch,
sagt Maria zu Josef,
als wir noch zu zweit waren,
hat uns das Christfest
nicht die Bohne interessiert.

Bei Jesus,
sagt Josef zu Maria,
da gebe ich dir recht!
Der kleine Bengel hat unser Leben
ganz schön verändert.

THREESOME

Isn't it funny,
says Mary to Joseph,
how we never cared much
about Christmas
when there were just the two of us?

Be Jaysus,
you're right,
says Joseph to Mary,
that little brat has certainly
changed our lives!

TRÍONÓIDÍN

Nach ait an obair é,
arsa Muire le hIósaf,
níor bhacamar
leis an Nollaig mórán
nuair nach raibh ann
ach an bheirt againn.

Dar Cníops,
tá an ceart agat,
ambaiste, tá an dailtín sin tar éis
an saol ar fad a athrú orainn!

Originally written in English, 'Threesome' is translated by the author into German, and into Irish by **Gabriel Rosenstock**

Wendy Cope

A POEM ABOUT JESUS

When I find myself feeling sorry for the wrong people –
disgraced MPs, vilified bankers,
the victims of paedophile witch-hunts –
I remember that Jesus was the friend of sinners
and he would have felt sorry for them too.

I love him for that. And I love him
for being on the side of the wusses,
telling us the meek will inherit the earth.

I don't know if he was the son of God.
I don't know if he rose from the grave.
If he is fiction,
the genius who created him
deserves all the love and the praise we can give.

Murray Bodo

WHITE BIRCH

Like a painting we almost see
Ourselves in, are You, O Christ:
A landscape, for example,
By Corot, the way white paint

Almost breaks the plain of trees
Dark against the distant view.
We're the child in the red hat,
You, O Lord, are the white birch

Starting to light the dark wood.
It almost becomes the One
The red-hat child turns to see
As if the child were us and we

Were in the silent painting and
You were what paint can't be.

Colum McCann

NAME AND NATURE: WHO DO YOU SAY THAT I AM?

My father was, or rather is, a rosarian. For decades he raised and bred roses in the back garden of our suburban home on Clonkeen Rd in Dublin. He spent much of his time in a small greenhouse at the rear of the garden, puttering about with seedlings and soil and secateurs. In the winter he dragged a kerosene heater to the greenhouse. In summer he opened the glass panels wide. Every day he walked down the lawn, in his flat hat and gloves, absorbed and intent. We had about seven hundred roses in our small garden. Miniatures, hybrid teas, floribundas, climbers. Sometimes he talked to them. He was adamant that the ones he talked to grew better, with strong colour, good foliage. If they took, he would name them. So many things in this world refuse naming, but not his roses: Sally Mac, Bloomsday, Isabella, Loretta's Rose, Kiss 'n Tell, Brightness.

In summertime the garden blazed with colour. In winter he went out and pruned the roses back so the garden was young and stark.

I admired him immensely, but I disliked working with the roses. I seldom worked the garden. I didn't mix the potting soil. I never learned how to breed the seeds. Occasionally I ran the lawnmower, but that was about it.

Twice a year, huge piles of manure arrived from the local farms for my brothers to fertilise the ground. Once, my pitchfork revealed a tiny baby calf. The contours of the world were complicated: even the garden was brought to life by death.

My father was at ease in his garden. The work was in compliance with beauty. The rest of the world – his job in a national newspaper, the pressures of raising a large family , the economics of the times – seemed to disappear, and often when I looked out the kitchen window to search for him I could not see him. He was most likely bent down to one of his seedlings, or dumping the new-mown grass at the bottom of the hedges, or in the rear shed preparing the spray for the greenfly (there were so many tasks to a simple hobby), but in later years it struck me that really he had become part of the landscape, *of* it and *in* it.

Once, in the early 1970s, when my sister answered the door, there was a man on our doorstep asking for our father. She said he was busy. The man insisted. He was there to collect a payment, or make a demand of some sort. Where was my father? he asked again. My sister, before gently closing the door, said again that he was busy. But busy where? said the man with his foot in the door. He was, said my sister, down in the back garden, playing God.

My father is still alive and sharp. He is in his mid-eighties. However, he can't work the garden any more. Most of the roses are gone, ploughed up, replaced by lawn and patio, but there are still a few around, in pots at the back of the house, a few in flowerbeds, and every now and then he likes to take his wheelchair into the back garden and wander down amongst them, taking joy in their presence.

He can still be seen talking to them, but I have no idea what it is that he says. Nor, frankly, do I want to know. Sometimes we have to allow mystery, no matter how small, to grow around us.

Michael Glover

THE BIRTH

All that needs to be done shall be done.
With the single star standing over,
Solemnity will attend upon the presentation
Of the treasures by the potentates.

Meanwhile, shepherds will blink awake
In the night, and a certain fearsome glory
Will lead them hurryingly down,
Stubbing their bleeding toes as they stumblingly go,

To a cow byre's homely stink, where a bundled child
Will have the fine-wrought shells of its tiny ears
Cocked to multitudes in the God-gracious heavens above,
Which shall be daubed all over with singing.

Michael Glover

THIS MAN

This man comes along.
He steals the breath from my body.
He scoops the pulsing from my heart.
He leaves me here, in the midst of nowhere.

This man comes along.
He snatches the questions from my mouth.
He wipes the last smile from my face.
He toys with my childish likeness.

This man comes along.
He builds a scaffold for himself.
He climbs up it.
He hangs down from it awkwardly, crying:

Just look at me now, familiar stranger.

Michael Glover

IN THE IMMEDIATE AFTERMATH

In the immediate aftermath, the enraged passerby
Removed the cross beam with his own bare hands –
One wrench and it was free. Lifting it on his shoulder,
He hurled it then straight down the hill.
They saw it roll, and hit a rock.

The Man himself was propped against a low wall,
Saying nothing, doing nothing, as good as
Dead to the world. The women were fussing,
Bringing him water, tamping at his wounds with rags.
He paid no attention to this at all.

His eyes were closed, his head slumped forward.
We could see the blood mingled with the greasy hair.
He wanted to say something, but he had no words,
Just a fierce tingling in his hands
From the pressure of all that brute wood and metal.

Michael Glover

CARELESSLY CAREFUL

Give no thought to the words that you will use.
The words will choose themselves.
Give no thought to your clothing either.
Your eyes will open, and you will be standing upright
In the chamber, appropriately dressed.

When they accuse you, both look at them
And do not look at them.
There is much beyond their hatred to admire:
The beauty of the desert sands stretching away;
A cup of water raised up in the midst of that desert.

When they enumerate your crimes,
Say over to yourself your ABC,
The one your mother used to sing to you beside the cradle.
She will be there for you, smiling.
And again, when you hang suspended.

She will hold you when they bring you down.
She will wrap you.
You will want for nothing.

Michael Glover

THE DECISION

I ask you to seize this man,
And cause him to suffer all due punishments,
Those of the day and of the night.
It is mete and right it shall be so.
He has stood out against us all these months.

You say he has little clothing.
Such clothing as he has remove from him.
Now plait a circlet of barbed wire,
And drag that length of sacking out,
The one that muffles the wind at the door's foot.

Adorn him with such stuff.
Listen to nothing that he says.
He has said enough, and more than once.
Too many mouths gape when he opens his.
Let his mouth be stopped once and for all.

There is his kingdom, the one that spins in his head,
And then there is ours, of flesh and blood,
Protected by all of you, my precious armoured men.
Now set to. Any hesitation on your part
Could be punished with death. Would you wish to join him?

Michael Glover

JESUS IS LORD

Imagine a column raised up tall in the desert
Topped by its capital, Doric, Corinthian or Ionic.

See the caravanserai sullenly approaching,
And how the traders whisper amongst themselves
Of its significance
As they make their slow encirclement.

The decision once made,
Watch how the dynamite reduces it
To a heap of dust
Amidst cheers and secret forebodings,

And how, as new morning approaches,
Its long shadow is seen to be returning,
To general consternation.

Observe how they build ramshackle shops against it,
Lean into it, smoking,
And, in time, gently ignore it.

Yes, Jesus surely is Lord.

Michael Glover

DEPENDING

This is the plain, unvarnished truth, Theophilus,
Which we witnessed with our eyes,
Of which I shall write to you in my own hand.
It is trembling, as if to say:
Believe me now, my friend.
You need never believe me again.

He came amongst us, as I shall declare,
Nothing to many, all to some.
He was nothing but a man amongst men.
And yet he was also set apart from us,
As if knowing from whence he came.
The Gadarene swine fled from him,
Plunging down the cliffs.
The very authorities feared him
For the weapon of his tongue.
They plotted. They decided.
They hung him up.
Wresting himself free,
He is amongst us now,
And forever more shall be.

This is all that I must write to you now ...
Dearest of friends, please listen.
So much depends.

Vincent Woods

ABOUT HIS BUSINESS

When he left school he worked on the farm –
Cut turf, saved hay, bushed gaps, set spuds,
Snagged turnips, put out manure.

His father beat him but only on a Friday.

Once he ran away to the town,
Slept in a ditch for two nights.

When his parents found him he was in the fair green
Surrounded by people all listening to him.
They said he was the smartest lad ever came about
And he should be let out more often,

The three of them went home and sat round the hob:
His mother fed him currant cake, his father stared at him
And said, 'To think that our boy could talk like that –
Well, it's fret.' Then they were silent

And sat late into the night.

from 'The Life and Miracles of Christy McGaddy',
first published in the collection *Lives and Miracles* (Arlen House, 2002)

Tim Liardet

SELF-PORTRAIT WITH SHROUD AND RADIATION GHOST

It's estimated tens of millions of volts were required
to burn the willowy ghost into the cloth. It was the radiation

scorched into the raw herringbone where it fell in its folds upon
the features of a man: here where the bony knee-joint

was slightly raised, here the bruised eyelid, the line of the mouth
and hands which rested gently in the groin – I want to touch

the weft of it, hold it to my cheek in its forty-eight folds,
place a finger through each hole where the boiling incense dripped

through the mite-infested fibres, and smouldered a hole,
found nothing at all the other side. As my finger pushes in first

through this hole, then this hole, then this, whatever percentage
of it passes through, disappears. Withdrawn again, it is whole.

The burns – the charred marks – of thermal radiation take a second
to form, a second, a thousand years, to disappear. The burns

are disappearing into the dark cloth. I want to lift it,
to hold it to my mouth to see if it is rough, or soft, or if it drops

to ash. To ash. Though palpable, the image is precarious
and not light-stable. As the cloth around it which remains uncharred

darkens as if to merge into night – though science tries to drag back
the scorched ghost, though I half try to hold it, half let it go –

though mouths which were emptied of them
now fill with ashes – though the Atheist starts to speak once more

in the first person plural and my father twenty years dead
must die once, die twice – all we have's a ripped rag.

Fiona Sampson

THE FOUR-LIMBED CROSS

Radiance lies along the arm
of the man asleep on a terrace
high above a lake, a shoreline and trees,

each of them fuzzy with heat.
The siesta world lies asleep
in its own arms. The sleeping man dreams

the dusty hillside is a holy mountain …
he sneezes, making a fly jump from his shoulder.
Somewhere below a goat coughs, a dog barks

as if in answer, and now his eyes open,
he struggles upright. Can't touch the sun –
though he blinks, imagining that once he did –

but lifts the jug of water at his feet,
making gold waver and run down both arms.

*

Water cools his throat. Shade cools his back.
He's learnt that though the beast he wears is simple,
wearing it is not. The beast scratches
and yawns. He'd like to tickle its toes

but the God-head in him won't stoop to that.
The God-head thinks the tree and the water
are metaphors for Father and Spirit.
The man knows only a spirit made of Nothing

could be so stupid. Incarnation sweats
and whines through the Mediterranean heat
where an olive tree and a well
are miracles of mud and water

moved by human will: as will moves
in him – its pressure in the throat like joy.

*

Joy surprises him, the way it will –
how pertinent it feels, how personal.
You could almost believe you'd been chosen

he thinks, walking uphill into sunset.
On either side, the hillside settles down
to a chorus of cicadas. A child

calls out – laughter – the smell of wood-smoke –
and it comes again, the tightening sense
that just being here is absolute

and, bound into the circle of his span,
he's touching all of it, stars and soil
stuffed like dirt beneath his fingernails.

I'm king of the hill, he starts to hum,
king of the hill. King of everything.

*

He feels his body is a kind of hum,
cornering him with gossip and reports
when he wants to concentrate. Thought
must be fired through synapses, with sparks

from the hormone boiler in the belly,
so it comes fitfully. Bread and wine
make it flare into understanding –
briefly. He wishes he could set it free

the way it seems to be in dreams and stories:
the way he seems to remember pure thought,
unendingly clear, and cold as a winter night –
as cold and clear as the high stars in winter –

Sometimes he longs to be nothing but spirit,
out of the hum of commonality.

*

He often wonders what they have in common –
these faces, raised to him like signs of trust.
Gazing is a sacrament. They open
up to him. Their open hearts are wounds,

tears clot their eyes. Liquid bodies
like their liquid souls: easily spilt.
Yet each makes his or her own loving contract

with the Leader that they see in him.
He wears their love like coronation robes
and feels himself stirred. His cock
twitches as he speaks. Being human,

he finds love suddenly moves him
and he wants to break himself open
to receive it all. To be let in.

*

Half god, half beast, he stumbles between the trees:
what use now are good looks, or charisma?
The human body is a poor, torn thing

always facing west towards its death.
Behind him the sun's about to bruise the lip
of the hill … He dare not look up.

What gets begun has to be finished,
and the dust beneath his feet is flowing
like a river towards the breaking shore.

He grips a branch as if to float
above the debris of his broken life,
but there's no anchor against mortality,

this body he'd begun to love, that shakes
and sweats, that seems to love – and betrays him.

Nate Klug

MARY MAGDALENE

What works against
the wish to blink, or check constantly back

over your right shoulder

that the world, supposed,
still holds there

with its dumb questions, its man
in muddied overalls

to whom you'd spoken,

turned, but who kept speaking
in this interval chiseling open,

brightness where his face had been
and a strange home

in the sound of your name

Dennis O'Driscoll

UPDATE

God, I still miss you some days,
fondly recall our happier times.
You used to take me into
your confidence, while I
fessed up to my transgressions,
owned up to grievous flaws.
And, granted absolution, I would
ascend to cloud nine,
mind on higher things,
ears only for your voice that conversed,
not in our inarticulate vernacular
but through lapidary Latin,
plainchant, exultant motet.
I recall the wet cathedral evenings
when your fair-weather friends
had absented themselves,
and we settled down by the fire
of the votive candle shrine
for a heart-to-heart confab,
our conversation never flagging.

What a good listener you always were
to me, God. I so wish we had not quarrelled,
gone our separate ways, making
too big an issue of the Jesuitical
distinctions that divided us, failing
to see eye-to-eye on articles of faith.

I still watch out for news of you,
gossip column tattle, and – an obsessive
divorcee – track your movements, eager
to learn which lovers take my place,
what types you hang about with these days,
what you're up to elsewhere
as you expand your horizons,
establishing new branches of your empire,
propagating universes by the second.

And you must feel a loneliness
close to empty nest syndrome
now that so many of your
erstwhile acolytes have flown the coop,
escaped your cage, questioned
your discretion, no longer prepared
to submit to your rough justice,
remain prisoners of your conscience.

God, how much I miss the comfort food
of your home-baked communion host.
And hush. The megaphones roped
to the telegraph poles relay around
the town your May procession:
The blue-gowned Child of Mary
women join with the choir.
The petal-strewing schoolgirls,
the banner-carrying sodality men,
and the canopy-bearing deacons
– custodians of the fragile Marian shrine
buoyant on its wildflower-brimming float –
break into song, give 'full-throated' voice
to the humming fecundity of early summer.

The year, refurbished, kitted out afresh,
is soaking up warm pastel colours,
reaching perfect pitch, oozing
through rejuvenated fields
a slow sempiternal note.

Notes on Contributors

Gillian Allnutt's eighth collection, *indwelling*, was published in 2013 by Bloodaxe Books. Earlier collections include *Nantucket and the Angel* (1997) and *Lintel* (2001), also from Bloodaxe; both books were shortlisted for the T S Eliot Prize. *Lintel* was a Poetry Book Society Choice. *How the Bicycle Shone: New and Selected Poems* was published in 2007.

Michael Augustin was born in Lübeck, Germany. He is a poet, broadcaster, translator and co-director of 'Poetry on the Road', Bremen's international literature festival. *Mickle Makes Muckle* (2007), a selection of his poems, mini-plays and miniatures in English translation is available from Dedalus Press. He is married to the poet Sujata Bhatt.

Ned Balbo's third book, *The Trials of Edgar Poe and Other Poems* (Story Line Press, 2010), received the 2012 Poets' Prize, and the 2010 Donald Justice Prize awarded by judge A E Stallings. *Lives of the Sleepers* (University of Notre Dame Press, 2005) received the Ernest Sandeen Poetry Prize and a ForeWord Book of the Year Gold Medal. *Galileo's Banquet* (Washington Writers' Publishing House, 1998) shared the Towson University Prize for Literature. He has received the Robert Frost Foundation Poetry Award and the John Guyon Literary Nonfiction Prize, and he is co-winner of the 2013 Willis Barnstone Translation Prize. He lives in Baltimore, Maryland.

Wendell Berry is an American man of letters, academic, cultural and economic critic, and farmer. He is a prolific author of novels, short stories, poems, and essays. He is also an elected member of the Fellowship of Southern Writers, a recipient of The National Humanities Medal, and the Jefferson Lecturer for 2012. *A Timbered Choir: The Sabbath Poems* 1979-1997 was published by Counterpoint in 1998.

Sujata Bhatt was born in India and grew up there and in the USA. She received her MFA from the Writers' Workshop at the University of Iowa. She is the author of eight collections of poetry, including a *Selected Poems* (1977) and a *Collected Poems* (2013), all from Carcanet Press. She divides her time between Germany and elsewhere.

Murray Bodo is a Franciscan Priest. His latest book is *Francis and Jesus* (Franciscan Media, 2013). His most recent book of poems is *Something Like Jasmine* (Tau Publishing, 2012). Fr. Murray lives in inner-city Cincinnati, Ohio, and spends two months of the year in Rome and Assisi as a staff member of 'Franciscan Pilgrimage Programs'.

Eva Bourke was born in Germany and has lived for many years in Galway. She has published several collections of her own work, the most recent being *piano* (Dedalus Press, 2011). She edited a major dual-language English / German anthology of Irish poetry, *In Green Ink / Mit Grüner Tinte*, and has translated into English the poetry of Elisabeth Borchers in *Winter on White Paper*. With Borbála Faragó, she edited *Landing Places: Immigrant Poets in Ireland* (Dedalus Press, 2010). She is a member of Aosdána.

John Burnside was born in 1955 in Dunfermline, Scotland, and now lives in Fife. He is a former Writer in Residence at Dundee University and now teaches at the University of St Andrews. He has won many awards for his poetry, including the Geoffrey Faber Memorial Prize and the Whitbread Poetry Award. Additionally, in 2011 his most recent collection, *Black Cat Bone*, published by Jonathan Cape, won both the Forward Poetry Prize and the T S Eliot Prize.

Paddy Bushe was born in Dublin, 1948. His poetry collections include *The Nitpicking of Cranes* (2004) and *To Ring in Silence: New and Selected Poems* (2008), both from Dedalus Press. His latest collection is *My Lord Buddha of Carraig Éanna* (Dedalus Press, 2012). The recipient of the Oireachtas prize for poetry in 2006, Paddy Bushe was also the recipient of the 2006 Michael Hartnett Poetry Award and was a runner-up for the Patrick Kavanagh award in 1988. He lives in Co Kerry.

Gillian Clarke was born in Cardiff, and is a poet, playwright, editor, broadcaster, lecturer and translator (from Welsh). In 2008 Clarke was appointed National Poet of Wales and in 2010 she was awarded the Queen's Gold Medal for Poetry. Carcanet Press publish her *Selected Poems* and *Collected Poems*, as well as her many poetry collections, including *Making the Beds for the Dead* (2004) and *A Recipe for Water* (2009). Her prose memoir *At the Source: A Writer's Year* was published in 2008. Her latest poetry collection *Ice* was shortlisted for the T S Eliot Prize in 2012.

Harry Clifton was born in 1952, now lives in Dublin and has been Ireland Professor of Poetry. He is a member of Aosdána. His most recent collection of poetry, *The Winter Sleep of Captain Lemass*, comes from Bloodaxe Books and Wake Forest University Press (2012).

Wendy Cope was a London primary school teacher until the publication of her first book of poems, *Making Cocoa for Kingsley Amis*, in 1986. Since then she has been a freelance writer. *Two Cures for Love*, a selection from her first three books of poems, appeared in 2008. Her fourth collection, *Family Values*, was published in 2011. She has also written for children and edited several anthologies. She lives in Ely, Cambridgeshire.

Robert Cording teaches English and creative writing at the College of the Holy Cross where he is the Barrett Professor of Creative Writing. He has published six collections of poems, including *Against Consolation* (CavanKerry Press, 2002); *Common Life* (CavanKerry Press, 2006); and his latest, *Walking With Ruskin* (CavanKerry, 2010).

Neil Curry was born in Newcastle upon Tyne and now lives in Ulverston in the Lake District. Enitharmon Press has published his four collections: *Ships in Bottles* (1988), a Poetry Book Society Recommendation; *Walking to Santiago* (1992); *The Bending of the Bow* (1993); and *The Road to the Gunpowder House* (2003). In 2007 Enitharmon also published his *Other Rooms: New and Selected poems*. He has completed a full-length study of William Cowper, to be published later this year.

Pádraig J Daly was born in Dungarvan, Co Waterford, and is now working as an Augustinian priest in Dublin. He has published several collections of poetry, among them *The Last Dreamers: New and Selected Poems* (1999), *Clinging to the Myth* (2007) and *Afterlife* (2010), all from Dedalus Press.

Dragan Dragojlović was born in Pilica, near Bajina Bašta, Serbia. He has published many books of poetry, including *The Book of Love and other poems of Love* (2008), *Traces of Our Lives* (2010), and *On the Squares of Babylon* (2010). He has also published novels and short stories, and edited a book of poetry by Yugoslav emigrants to the USA and Canada, *From Heart to Homeland* (1989). He translates poetry from English into Serbian, and is Director of the Ivo Andrić Foundation in Belgrade.

Steve Ely is an English poet from Yorkshire. His book, *Oswald's Book of Hours*, was published by Smokestack in 2013.

John Ennis is an author of thirteen books of poetry. His collection, *Postponing Ásbyrgi*, poems in response to Sìgur Rós, was published by Three Spires Press in 2013 and launched throughout Newfoundland at The March Hare Festival. Retired from education, Ennis is an activist and has been green-starred for his contribution to Amnesty International.

Michael Glover is a Sheffield-born, London-based poet, editor and art critic. His most recent books were *Only So Much* (poetry) and *Headlong into Pennilessness* (a memoir of growing up in Sheffield), both published in 2011.

James Harpur has had five books of poetry published by Anvil Press, including his latest, *Angels and Harvesters* (2012), a Poetry Book Society Recommendation. He is a poetry editor, adjudicator and workshop facilitator and is currently poetry editor of the *Temenos Academy Review*. He lives in West Cork.

David Harsent has published nine volumes of poetry. *Legion* (Faber and Faber) won the Forward Prize for best collection in 2005; *Night* (Faber and Faber, 2011) was triple-shortlisted in the UK and won the Griffin International Poetry Prize. *In Secret*, his English translation of poems by Yannis Ritsos, was published by Enitharmon Press in 2012 in the UK, and in 2013 in the USA. He is Professor of Creative Writing at the University of Roehampton.

Seamus Heaney was born in 1939 in Derry/Londonderry. *Death of a Naturalist*, his first collection, appeared in 1966. In the early 1960s he became a lecturer in Belfast after attending university there. He lived in Sandymount, Dublin from 1972 until his death. He was a professor at Harvard from 1981 to 1997 and its Poet in Residence from 1988 to 2006. From 1989 to 1994 he was also the Professor of Poetry at Oxford. He was awarded the 1995 Nobel Prize in Literature. Other awards that Heaney received include the Geoffrey Faber Memorial Prize (1968), the E M Forster Award (1975), the PEN Translation Prize (1985), the Golden Wreath of Poetry (2001), T S Eliot Prize (2006) and two Whitbread Prizes (1996 and 1999). In 2012, he was awarded the Lifetime Recognition Award from the Griffin Trust For Excellence In Poetry. He died in Dublin in August 2013.

Mark Patrick Hederman is Abbot of Glenstal Abbey, a Benedictine monastery, in Limerick, Ireland.

Andrew Hudgins is the author of many books of poems, including *Saints and Strangers* (Houghton Mifflin, 1985), *The Glass Hammer* (Houghton Mifflin, 1994), and most recently *A Clown at Midnight* (Mariner Books, 2013). He has been a finalist for the National Book Award and the Pulitzer Prize, is a recipient of Guggenheim and National Endowment for the Arts fellowships, as well as the Harper Lee Award. He currently teaches in the Department of English at Ohio State University.

Mark Jarman is the author of *Bone Fires: New and Selected Poems*, published by Sarabande Books in 2011. He has also published two books of essays about poetry, *The Secret of Poetry* (Story Line Press, 2001) and *Body and Soul: Essays on Poetry* (University of Michigan Press, 2002). He is Centennial Professor of English at Vanderbilt University.

George Kalogeris received a master's degree in creative writing from Boston University in 1986. He completed his Ph.D. studies in comparative literature at the University Professors Program, Boston University in 1991. His doctoral thesis was entitled 'Folk Songs and Foreign Influences in Modern Greek Poetry: the Growth of the Demotic Tradition'. His poems have appeared in *Agni*, *Harvard Review* and *Ploughshares*. 'Horace in Athens', translated from Cavafy, appears in *Horace in English* (Penguin, 1996).

Thomas Kinsella was born in Dublin in 1928. His awards and honours include Guggenheim Fellowships, the Denis Devlin Memorial Award, the Irish Arts Council Triennial Book Award and honorary doctorates from the University of Turin and the National University of Ireland. In 2007 Thomas Kinsella was awarded the Freedom of the City of Dublin. Carcanet Press publish several of his books including *The Dual Tradition* and *Collected Poems*. In 2013 Carcanet published his last five Peppercanister booklets under the title *Late Poems*.

Nate Klug's work has appeared in *Poetry*, *The Threepenny Review* and in many other journals. *Rude Woods*, passages from Virgil's *Eclogues*, appeared in 2013 from The Song Cave. He currently lives in central Iowa.

Andrew Lansdown is a widely published, award-winning, Australian writer who has published novels, short story collections, children's poetry and poetry collections. His latest poetry collections are *Far from Home: Poems of Faith, grief and gladness* (Wombat Books, 2010); *The Colour of Life*, in the book *Two Poets* (Fremantle Press, 2011); and *Inadvertent Things: Poems in traditional Japanese forms* (Walleah Press, 2013).

Stanislava Lazarević is the translator of Dragan Dragojlović's collection *Death's Homeland*, published by Curbstone Press in 2008.

Gwyneth Lewis was National Poet of Wales 2005-06. Her latest book is *Sparrow Tree* (Bloodaxe Books, 2011), which won the Roland Mathias Prize 2012. Her two memoirs are *Sunbathing in the Rain* (Flamingo, 2002) and *Two in a Boat* (Fourth Estate, 2005).

Tim Liardet has produced seven collections of poetry. *The Storm House*, his latest collection, was published by Carcanet Press in 2011. His next full collection, *Portrait in the Gaudi Mirror*, is due from Carcanet in 2015; and his *New and Selected Poems*, from the same publisher, is due in 2016. He is Professor of Poetry at Bath Spa University.

Michael Longley was born in Belfast, and was Professor of Poetry for Ireland from 2007 to 2010, a cross-border academic post set up in 1998. He has published many collections of poetry, among them *Gorse Fires* (Wake Forest University Press, 1991) which won the Whitbread Poetry Prize, and *The Weather in Japan* (Wake Forest University Press, 2000), which won the T. S. Eliot Prize and the Hawthornden Prize. He was the 2001 recipient of the Queen's Gold Medal for Poetry. His most recent collection, *A Hundred Doors*, won the Poetry Now Award in September 2012.

Colum McCann was born in Ireland in 1965. He is the author of six novels and two collections of stories. He has been the recipient of many international honours, including the National Book Award and the International IMPAC Dublin Literary Award. He teaches at the MFA programme in Hunter College, New York.

Patricia McCarthy, winner of The Poetry Society's National Poetry Competition 2013, is the editor of the poetry journal *Agenda*. After Trinity College, Dublin, she lived in Washington D.C., Paris, Bangladesh, Nepal and Mexico. She has lived now for more than two decades in Mayfield, East Sussex, where she taught English for fifteen years. Her collection, *Rodin's Shadow* (Clutag Press / Agenda Editions) came out in 2012. *Around the Mulberry Bush: New and Selected Poems* is forthcoming from Waterloo Press. *Horses Between Our Legs*, a sequence of poems glancing off World War I and headed by her National Poetry Competition winning poem, is due out also at the end of this year.

Thomas McCarthy has published seven collections with Anvil Press, including *Merchant Prince* (2005) and *The Last Geraldine Officer* (2009). He is a former recipient of the Lawrence O'Shaughnessy Award for Poetry of the Centre for Irish Studies at the University of St Thomas, Minnesota.

Enda McDonagh was born in Bekan, Co Mayo and is a priest of the Archdiocese of Tuam. He studied in Maynooth, and was awarded a Doctorate in Divinity. He received a Doctorate in Canon Law in Munich. He was appointed Professor of Moral Theology and Canon in 1958, a post which he held until his retirement from full time teaching in 1995. He was president of the National Conference of priests in Ireland and was official chaplain to Mary Robinson during her presidency. He has published many articles on art and on poetry, making a special study of poetry in the context of faith, particularly in *Vulnerable to the Holy* (2005) and *Theology in Winter Light* (2010), both from Columba Press.

Philip McDonagh has served as Ireland's ambassador to India, the Holy See, Finland, and the Russian Federation, and he is is currently Permanent Representative to the Organisation for Security and Cooperation in Europe. He has published four volumes of poetry, including *The Song The Oriole Sang* (Dedalus Press, 2010), while his essays have appeared in *Poetry Ireland Review*, *Studies*, *Logos* and the *India International Quarterly*.

Conor McDonough OP is a student brother in the Irish Province of Dominicans, based in St Saviour's priory in Dublin. He is from Galway and was educated in St Mary's College, Galway and King's College, Cambridge.

Maitreyabandhu has won the Keats-Shelley Prize, the Basil Bunting Award, the Geoffrey Dearmer Prize, and the Ledbury Festival Poetry Competition. His first full-length collection *The Crumb Road* (Bloodaxe, 2013) is a Poetry Book Society Recommendation. He lives and works in the London Buddhist Centre.

Fred Marchant has published four poetry collections: *Tipping Point*, published by The Word Works, won the 1993 Washington Prize; *House on Water, House in Air* was published by Dedalus Press in 2002; *Full Moon Boat* appeared from Graywolf in 2000; and *The Looking House* appeared in 2009 from the same publisher. Marchant is Director of the Creative Programme and The Poetry Centre at Suffolk University, Boston, Massachusetts.

Sinéad Morrissey collections are *There Was Fire in Vancouver* (1996), *Between Here and There* (2002), *The State of the Prisons* (2005), *Through the Square Window* (2009), and the Forward Prize-shortlisted *Parallax* (2013), all published by Carcanet Press. *Parallax* won the 2014 T S Eliot prize. She lectures in creative writing at the Seamus Heaney Centre for Poetry, Queen's University, Belfast, and is Belfast's inaugural Poet Laureate.

Paul Murray is a Dominican priest working in Rome where he teaches the literature of the mystical tradition. His latest work in prose is *Aquinas at Prayer: The Bible, Mysticism and Poetry* (Bloomsbury, 2013). He has published four collections of poems, the last two, *The Absent Fountain* and *These Black Stars*, with Dedalus Press. These have recently been re-published in a single volume: *Stones and Stars*.

Eiléan Ní Chuilleanáin was educated at University College, Cork, and Oxford. She is a poet and Emeritus Fellow of Trinity College, Dublin, where she has taught since 1966. Her *Selected Poems* was published by Gallery Press and Faber and Faber in 2008; her latest book, *The Sun-Fish*, was short-listed for the T S Eliot Prize and was awarded the Griffin International Prize for Poetry in 2010.

John O'Donnell's poetry has been published and broadcast widely. His awards include the Hennessy / *Sunday Tribune* Award, the Ireland Funds Prize and the Irish National Poetry Prize. He has published two collections: *Some Other Country* (Bradshaw Books, 2002) and *Icarus Sees His Father Fly* (Dedalus Press, 2004). His latest collection of poetry, *On Water*, is forthcoming from Dedalus Press.

Dennis O'Driscoll was born in Thurles in 1954, and published many books of poetry with Anvil Press, including *New and Selected Poems* (2004), a Poetry Book Society Special Commendation; *Reality Check* (2007); and *Dear Life* (2012), winner of the Irish Times Poetry Now Award. His book, *Stepping Stones: Interviews with Seamus Heaney* (Faber and Faber 2008), was shortlisted for 'Book of the Decade' in the Irish Book Awards 2010. He was a member of Aosdána and an Honorary Member of the Royal Hibernian Academy, and was awarded an honorary doctorate in literature by University College Dublin in 2009. Dennis O'Driscoll died in December 2012.

Ruth Padel is a London-based poet and a Fellow of the Royal Society of Literature. She has published eight collections, most recently the lyric biography of her great-great-grandfather Charles Darwin, *Darwin – A Life in Poems* (Vintage, 2009), shortlisted for the Costa Prize; and *The Mara Crossing* (Chatto and Windus, 2012), poems and prose on migration, shortlisted for the Ted Hughes Award. Tring Chamber Music, for their 2013 Easter Concert, commissioned her to write poems to be read between the movements of Josef Haydn's quartet *Seven Last Words of Christ on the Cross*. The sequence will be published in her forthcoming collection *Learning to Make an Oud in Nazareth* (Chatto and Windus, 2014). Ruth is currently blogging on Faust and the devil for the Royal Opera House, Covent Garden at www.ruthpadel.com/blog.

Ian Parks's latest collection, *The Cavafy Variations* (Rack Press, 2013), is a Poetry Book Society Choice. He was writer in residence at Gladstone's Library in 2012 and is currently Writing Fellow at De Montfort University, Leicester.

Paul Perry is the author of numerous critically acclaimed books of poetry and fiction, including *Gunpowder Valentine: New and Selected Poems* which is due this year from Dedalus Press, and *The Innocent Sleep*, a 'Karen Perry' thriller published by Penguin UK and Holt USA. He is Associate Professor of Creative Writing and English Literature, and Director of the MFA in Creative Writing at Kingston University, London, and Fellow in Creative Writing at UCD.

John Poch is Professor of English at Texas Tech University. He is the author of three collections of poems, most recently *Dolls* (Orchises Press, 2009).

Gabriel Rosenstock's latest titles include a new bilingual selection *Margadh na Míol in Valparaíso/ The Flea Market in Valparaíso*, selected and introduced by Cathal Ó Searcaigh with translations by Paddy Bushe (Cló Iar-Chonnacht, 2014), and *The Partisan and others stories* (Evertype 2014).

Armand Garnet Ruffo draws on his Ojibway heritage for much of his writing. Born and raised in northern Ontario, Canada, he lives in Ottawa and teaches at Carleton University. His new collection *The Thunderbird Poems* will be published in 2014 by Insomniac Press.

Fiona Sampson has published more than twenty books of poetry, criticism and philosophy of language. She has twice been shortlisted for both the T S Eliot and Forward Prizes. She is the Editor of *Poem* and Professor of Poetry at the University of Roehampton, where she directs the Poetry Centre. In 2013 she published *Coleshill* (Chatto) and, in the US, *Night Fugue: Selected Poems* (Sheep Meadow Press).

Penelope Shuttle's collection *Sandgrain and Hourglass* appeared from Bloodaxe Books in 2010, and was a Recommendation of The Poetry Book Society, and a Poetry Book of the Year in the *Financial Times*. *Unsent: New and Selected Poems* 1980-2012 was published in 2012 (Bloodaxe Books).

Gerard Smyth, born in Dublin, was managing editor of *The Irish Times* for several years. He is the author of eight poetry collections, the most recent being *The Mirror Tent* (2007) and *The Fullness of Time: New and Selected Poems* (2010), both from Dedalus Press. He is co-editor with Pat Boran of *If Ever You Go: A Map of Dublin in Poetry and Song* (Dedalus Press), the Dublin: One City One Book title for 2014.

Pauline Stainer is a freelance writer and tutor, and was selected for the 1994 New Generation Poets promotion. Several of her poetry collections were Poetry Book Society Recommendations. Bloodaxe Books published *The Lady and the Hare: New and Selected Poems* in 2003. A new collection, *Tiger Facing the Mist*, appeared from Bloodaxe in 2013.

Daniel Tobin is the author of five books of poems, most recently *Second Things* (Four Way Books, 2008), and *Belated Heavens* (Four Way Books, 2010). His critical study, *Passage to the Center: Imagination and the Sacred in the Poetry of Seamus Heaney*, came out from the University of Kentucky Press in 1999. He is Interim Dean of the School of the Arts at Emerson College in Boston.

William Wenthe's books of poetry are *Words Before Dawn* (LSU Press, 2012), *Not Till We Are Lost* (LSU Press, 2003) and *Birds of Hoboken* (Orchises Press, 1995). His poems have appeared in *Poetry, Paris Review, Georgia Review, Southern Review, Tin House, Poetry Daily*, among many other outlets; and he has received fellowships from the NEA, the Texas Commission on the Arts, and Pushcart Prizes. Born and raised in New Jersey, he teaches poetry at Texas Tech University.

Rowan Williams was born in South Wales and educated there and in Cambridge and Oxford. After several years of pastoral and academic work he became Bishop of Monmouth in 1992, Archbishop of Wales in 1999, and Archbishop of Canterbury in 2002. He returned to Cambridge as Master of Magdalene College at the beginning of 2013. A new poetry collection, *The Other Mountain*, is due this year from Carcanet Press.

Christian Wiman is a poet, translator and essayist. For several years he edited *Poetry*, a Chicago magazine. In 2013 he was appointed to the faculty of the Yale Institute of Sacred Music as Senior Lecturer in Religion and Literature. His collections from Copper Canyon Press are *The Long Home* (1998) and *Hard Night* (2005). *Every Riven Thing* was published by Farrar Strauss and Giroux in 2010; FSG also published his memoir/essay *My Bright Abyss: Meditation of a Modern Believer*, in 2013.

Vincent Woods is a playwright, poet and broadcaster. His radio play, *Broken Moon*, was broadcast on RTÉ Radio 1 in May, 2012. He is currently working on a third collection of poetry. He is a member of Aosdána.

Valentina Aleksandrovna Zhogova is a contemporary Russian iconographer. Born in Sergiyev Posad in 1989, she received an academic education in painting and drawing but now prefers a decorative style for which she has developed her own system of images and symbols, incorporating the paintings of the old masters, folk art and icon painting. Her work has been exhibited widely in Russia in recent years, including at the Exhibition of Diploma works for Abramtsevo Art College graduates, in the Moscow Kremlin, and for the Russian Union of Artists. The seven icons included in this issue are from her series illustrating a Calendar of Russian Folk Celebrations.

Former Editors of *Poetry Ireland Review*

John Jordan 1–8	Spring 1981–Autumn 1983
Thomas McCarthy 9–12	Winter 1983–Winter 1984
Conleth Ellis and Rita E Kelly 13	Spring 1985
Terence Brown 14–17	Autumn 1985–Autumn 1986
Ciaran Cosgrove 18–19	Spring 1987
Dennis O'Driscoll 20–21	Autumn 1987–Spring 1988
John Ennis and Rory Brennan 22–23	Summer 1988
John Ennis 24–25	Winter 1988–Spring 1989
Micheal O'Siadhail 26–29	Summer 1989–Summer 1990
Máire Mhac an tSaoi 30–33	Autumn 1990–Winter 1991
Peter Denman 34–37	Spring 1992–Winter 1992
Pat Boran 38	Summer 1993
Seán Ó Cearnaigh 39	Autumn 1993
Pat Boran 40–42	Winter 1993–Summer 1994
Chris Agee 43–44	Autumn/Winter 1994
Moya Cannon 45–48	Spring 1995–Winter 1995
Liam Ó Muirthile 49	Spring 1996
Michael Longley 50	Summer 1996
Liam Ó Muirthile 51–52	Autumn 1996–Spring 1997
Frank Ormsby 53–56	Summer 1997–Spring 1998
Catherine Phil MacCarthy 57–60	Summer 1998–Spring 1999
Mark Roper 61–64	Summer 1999– Spring 2000
Biddy Jenkinson 65–68	Summer 2000–Spring 2001
Maurice Harmon 69–72	Summer 2001–Spring 2002
Michael Smith 73–75	Summer 2002–Winter 2002
Eva Bourke 76	Spring/Summer 2003
Peter Sirr 77–91	Autumn 2003 / October 2007
Eiléan Ní Chuilleanáin 92–95	December 2007/October 2008
Caitríona O'Reilly 96–99	December 2008/October 2009
Paul Muldoon 100	March 2010
Caitríona O'Reilly 101–104	July 2010/September 2011
John F Deane 105-112	December 2011–April 2014